////////A GUIDE TO ////////
IMPROVISED WEAPONRY

HOW TO PROTECT YOURSELF WITH WHATEVER YOU'VE GOT

Master Sergeant **TERRY SCHAPPERT**, U.S. Army Special Forces
and **ADAM SLUTSKY**

Avon, Massachusetts

Published by
Adams Media, a division of F+W Media, Inc.
57 Littlefield Street, Avon, MA 02322. U.S.A.
www.adamsmedia.com

ISBN 10: 1-4405-8472-9
ISBN 13: 978-1-4405-8472-5
eISBN 10: 1-4405-8473-7
eISBN 13: 978-1-4405-8473-2

Printed in the United States of America.

10   9   8   7   6   5   4

Certain sections of the book deal with activities that may result in serious bodily harm or even death. The authors, Adams Media, and F+W Media, Inc. do not accept liability for any injury, loss, legal consequence, or incidental or consequential damage incurred by reliance on the information or advice provided in this book. The information in this book is for entertainment purposes only.

Cover design by Frank Rivera.
Cover images © iStockphoto.com/greenwatermelon.
Interior images © iStockphoto.com.

*This book is available at quantity discounts for bulk purchases.
For information, please call 1-800-289-0963.*

DEDICATION

To all the foreign enemies, street thugs, belligerent drunks,
and other assorted threats that have come my way—
thanks for keeping me on my toes, and my sincerest wishes
that you mend your ways or meet your maker.
—Terry Schappert

For Darla, Veronica, Sammi, Taylor, and Tracey—
I will *always* protect you.
—Adam Slutsky

ACKNOWLEDGMENTS

A huge *thank you* to the brave men and women of the United States Armed Forces who put life and limb on the line every moment of every day to protect this great nation of ours. The debt of gratitude we owe you and your families can never truly be repaid, only honored and respected.

Thanks also to our fantastic team at Adams Media, led by Tom Hardej; our editor extraordinaire Katie Corcoran Lytle; and to our incredible literary agent, Renée C. Fountain, at Gandolfo Helin.

CONTENTS

Introduction 7

The Green Beret Way 9

2 × 4 11
Aerosol Can 13
Ashtray. 15
Bag of Dog Poop 17
Barrette/Bobby Pin. 19
Baseball Cap. 21
Billfold/Wallet 23
Billiard Ball 25
Blanket. 27
Book of Matches 29
Bottle of Hot Sauce 30
Bouquet of Flowers 32
Bowling Ball. 34
Broom/Mop. 36
Candle 38
Candy Bar 40
Car Antenna. 42
Car Keys 44
Cellphone 46
Ceramic Plate. 48
Chain. 50

Chopsticks 52
Clipboard. 54
Coffee Mug 56
Coffeepot. 58
Comb (Plastic) 60
Corkscrew 61
Crutches. 63
Cue Stick 65
Dirty Diaper 67
Dish Soap. 69
Disposable Razor 70
Dog Leash 72
Drinking Straw 74
Duct Tape/Electrical Tape 76
Extension Cord 78
Eyeglasses/Sunglasses 80
Fire Extinguisher 82
Flashlight. 84
Fork (Metal). 86
Frisbee 88
Frying Pan 90

Garbage Can 92	Rearview Mirror.............. 151
Golf Bag..................... 94	Roll of Toilet Paper............ 153
Guitar 97	Rolling Pin (American Style) 155
Hairbrush.................... 99	Rope 157
Hammer 101	Rubber Band 159
Handful of Coins.............. 103	Safety Pin................... 161
High Heels.................. 105	Salad Tongs 163
Ice Scraper 107	Salt....................... 165
Jumper Cables 109	Scarf/Necktie 166
Laptop Computer 111	Scuba Tank.................. 167
Light Bulb 113	Seat Belt................... 169
Lighter 115	Shoehorn 171
Lipstick/Lip Balm 117	Shopping Cart 173
Mirror (Handheld)............. 119	Sneakers/Shoes............... 175
Nail File/Emery Board 121	Socks 177
Newspaper.................. 123	Staple Puller................. 179
Oven Mitt 125	T-shirt 181
Paper Clip 127	Takeout Container (with Food Inside) 183
Pen/Pencil 129	Thumbtacks................. 184
Pillow/Pillowcase 131	Toothbrush 186
Ping-Pong Paddle............. 133	Towel..................... 187
Pizza Box (with Pizza Inside) 135	Turkey Baster 188
Plastic Bag/Garbage Bag......... 137	TV Remote Control............ 190
Plunger 139	Tweezers................... 191
Pocketbook 141	Umbrella 193
Poker Chips/Casino Chips 143	Water Bottle................. 195
Powder Puff 145	Windshield Wiper 196
PVC Pipe.................. 147	Wire Coat Hanger 198
Quart of Oil................ 149	Wristwatch.................. 200

Afterword 202
Glossary of Terms 203
Index..204

INTRODUCTION

Did you ever think that you could use an oven mitt to defend yourself against a home invader? How about using a dirty diaper to fend off a mugger? Or a drinking straw to take down a terrorist?

Like it or not, we live in scary times. Violent crime is on the rise. Overcrowded jails and prisons are releasing scores of dangerous criminals prematurely. And the threat of another major terrorist attack within our borders is real. With this ever-present danger lurking at every turn, there's a chance that, at some point, you may be faced with a frank decision that every living organism has experienced since the dawn of time: fight or flight. When that frightening moment comes, shelve your ego immediately. If you can extricate yourself from a dicey situation simply by running away, do it! There's no shame in survival. However, if fleeing isn't an option—if you're forced to stand your ground—knowing how to defend yourself can make all the difference between life and death.

Equipped with that knowledge, if a confrontation is inevitable, you'd be wise to arm yourself. Even the smallest object is superior to the biggest fist. Fortunately, virtually any object—from a coffee mug to a rubber band to even your own sneakers—can be used as a weapon . . . if you know how to handle it correctly. Some items can be used exactly as they are, whereas others require some creative manipulation to be used in a defensive capacity. Granted, some of these objects and instructions may seem a bit peculiar, but there's a method to our madness. We've purposely taken an unconventional approach to improvised weaponry and self-defense in order to get you thinking, and to show you that no matter what the situation you're facing, there is always something you can do, and, in all likelihood, there is always something within reach to assist you.

In addition to the objects and their possible uses, we've included sidebars that clue you in regarding the psychology, mindset, and stark reality of having your life threatened and how to deal with that harsh scenario should such a situation arise. Please know that this book is not intended to scare you. Quite the opposite. We want to assure you that you have a chance—a *good* chance—of coming out on top of a bad situation, if you utilize the underestimated courage and ability you have lurking inside you, just by being the kind of person who can "flip that switch" when it's required.

Remember, you don't have to be a Green Beret or an MMA star to win a fight. You just need to have something to fight for; something, no matter how innocuous, to fight with; and the tenacity to not stop until the fight is over. As a matter of fact, the *less* you look like a badass, the more of an advantage you may have when some street thug sets his sights on you, only to realize too late that he picked the wrong prey—the prey that becomes the predator. And that philosophy doesn't only apply to self-defense, either. It's a philosophy you can benefit from in every aspect of your life. And it's that philosophy that will enable you to see every object around you, great or small, normal to obscure, as a potential weapon to be used against anyone threatening your safety.

THE GREEN BERET WAY

So how do we know how to protect ourselves in a fight? Where did we find out how to use all of these everyday items in ways that are completely unexpected—for both you and your possible attacker? Two words: Green Beret.

Green Berets like Terry Schappert are the multi-tools of the Special Operations community. The true "first in, last out" operatives, Green Berets are far more than merely weaponry-toting badasses. They are trainers, teachers, and advisers who go through extensive cultural and language training in order to truly immerse themselves in whichever foreign land they are dispatched to. They also receive additional specialized training in every category you can think of: medicine and trauma, engineering, computers . . . the list is endless. Green Berets have delivered babies; inoculated farm animals; pulled teeth; built homes and structures; blown up buildings; and trained, lead, and kicked down doors alongside host nations' soldiers. But even with all their skills and abilities, it's still not a cinch to pick a Green Beret out from a crowd. They're not (all) musclebound, Conan-looking freaks with "Death from Above" (or any other professional warrior motto) tattooed on their foreheads. Green Berets go out of their way to blend in, to hide in plain sight. And excessive use of action and force is never on the menu. Sure, when push comes to shove, these guys will stand and deliver, no questions asked. But they'd much prefer to accomplish their assigned tasks with as minimal effort and signature as possible. Bottom line: They aim to be ghosts. Very effective ghosts. In that respect, Green Berets are the ultimate problem solvers. They don't take no for an answer; and when they encounter resistance, they don't see a wall, but merely an obstacle that they must climb over, tunnel under, maneuver around or, if all else fails, go right freakin' through. The content of this book is a testament to that ideology. Don't panic. Weigh your options. Use all means necessary and all available tools. Solve the problem. Survive. Go home to your family. By applying that logic—and ultimately that determination—to any physical confrontation that comes your way, you will—at least in spirit—join the ranks of the illustrious United States Army Special Forces, the Green Berets.

GREEN BERET GUIDANCE

Green Berets and other members of the Special Ops or self-defense community use an array of terms that may not be familiar to someone just learning how to take down an attacker. If words like garrote, *kusari-fundo*, fist filler, or eskrima sticks leave you scratching your head, check out the glossary at the end of the book to make sure the self-defense objects and tactics described throughout make sense.

2 × 4

Scenario

You're walking past a construction site when a vagrant who has been making the unfinished structure his home accuses you of intruding on his turf. Next thing you know, the bum pulls a knife and is intent on sticking it in you.

What do you do?

Tactics

If you don't think you can outrun your attacker, head straight to the unused lumber pile and grab a 2 × 4. They come in different lengths and weights (depending on the type of wood), so choose one that's easy for you to wield with some degree of control. Once you have your 2 × 4, consider the following options:

1. Swing the 2 × 4 like a baseball bat. Don't choke up too far, though; you'll shorten the plank's contact length and decrease the range of effectiveness. Also, don't try to "hit a home run" by aiming for the head. The head is a small, fast-moving target that's hard to hit. Instead, aim for your opponent's extremities: legs (knees, shins, and feet) or arms (elbows, wrists, and hands).

2. Use the 2 × 4 like a prod. Hold the underside of the plank (palm up) with your weak hand (the hand you don't write or throw with) to steady it while your strong/dominant hand (the hand you do write or throw with) grasps one of the plank's ends. Now imagine the board (and the hand driving it) as a piston, and drive the

plank forward into your adversary. Aim for soft, sensitive targets like the groin or throat. The nose, jaw, and forehead are also vital areas to target.

3. Hold the 2 × 4 with both hands, sledgehammer style, to smash toes or, if you're standing above your enemy (on a ladder or balcony), on top of the head.

4. If you're being chased, try to gain some distance to separate from your attacker and, after rounding the nearest corner, extend the 2 × 4 past the corner at ankle level to trip him, or at face level to concuss him.

 GREEN BERET GUIDANCE

Special Operations Forces, the term given to the entirety of the U.S. military's elite commandos, is a distinguished category of which the Green Berets are a part. These commandos have one dozen essential requirements, referred to as the Special Operations Imperatives, which must be met for any mission to be considered a success. Specifically ordered, the number one imperative is: Know your operational environment. Translation: Always know what's around you and what kind of situation you're walking into. Going somewhere new? Do your homework. Is it a sketchy neighborhood? High crime rate? Do gangs inhabit the area? Any problems or political unrest lately? Also, be smart with your actions. For example, don't leave Walmart at 11 P.M. and have your nose buried in your smartphone while en route to your car. Avoid situations *before* they become situations.

AEROSOL CAN

Scenario

You're exiting a grocery store with a bag of groceries when a mugger decides your purchases should be *his* purchases. But the look in his eyes makes it abundantly clear that this creep is out for more than just food. Maybe it's your car, your wallet, your new cellphone, the snazzy watch on your wrist—heck, maybe it's your sunglasses. Whatever the case, he's looking to hurt someone and that someone is you!

What do you do?

Tactics

As luck would have it, the last item that went into your bag was an aerosol can (of hair spray, deodorant, cooking spray, bug spray, mechanical lubricant, degreaser, etc.). Granted, you may wish it was something a little more high powered, but since you weren't grocery shopping at Preppers Paradise, the aerosol can will just have to do.

Once you have your can in hand, consider the following:

1. The range of effectiveness of your aerosol will vary greatly depending on the contents of your can. If you have more than one type of aerosol can in your bag and the time to choose, select the one with the greatest range and/or the most potent contents. In most cases, you'll want to pick the can of insect spray over the hair spray, deodorant, or cooking spray.

2. Shake it vigorously and spray, aiming for your target's face in general, and the eyes in particular. The eyes aren't just the

windows to the soul—in self-defense speak they're the "keys to the kingdom." Take away your enemy's vision, and the battle is all but over. However, even if you hit your attacker square in the eyes, don't take that for granted. Not all substances will irritate enough to completely compromise vision, which means your attacker could still pose a threat. Be prepared to follow up with a punch or kick, or another improvised weapon. Treat the spray more like a distraction.

3. Use it as a flamethrower. Hold a burning match, lighter, or candle in front of the nozzle and spray. For one-handed operation, tape a candle in front of the nozzle. A candle designed for outdoor use with some resistance to wind is best, but if you're caught off-guard, use what you have on hand.

 EXPERT ADVICE

There is a myth that wasp spray is more effective than pepper spray for self-defense. You don't use salt if the recipe calls for sugar, and you don't use tennis balls to play golf. If you're looking for a nonlethal spray weapon for self-defense, choose a spray designed for that purpose.

ASHTRAY

Scenario

You're playing blackjack at your favorite casino and you're on a winning streak, stacking chips from your fourth 21 in a row. Unfortunately, your winning streak hits a dead end when the unlucky player seated next to you, who hasn't won a hand since you sat down, erupts at yet another loss and decides to take his frustration out on you.

What do you do?

Tactics

The martini glass in front of you is way too fragile to stake your safety on. That's when you notice the solid glass ashtray. With so many public anti-smoking laws in effect these days, finding an ashtray in a public venue is akin to finding a needle in a haystack. But smoking is still permitted in most casinos, and where there's smoking, there are ashtrays. This one may just save your life. Once you have the ashtray in hand, consider the following options:

1. If the ashtray has any robustness (a solid chunk of glass, for example), use it as an impact weapon. Grasp it tightly in your hand, and swing with the same motion you would use when swinging a hammer. Be careful not to palm any sharp edges. For best results, strike your enemy with the sharpest or thickest edge.

2. Target the hands or fingers, especially if your attacker has a hand on the table, or go for his toes if he's wearing soft shoes or sandals. You don't need much force to crush or sever a digit.

3. If an opportunity to strike your attacker's head presents itself, aim for the temple, the base of the skull, or directly behind the ear. A hard impact to any of these areas will likely put the offender down, even if drugs or alcohol have heightened his pain threshold or amped up his strength.

4. If you're looking to do some damage, jam the ashtray into the attacker's open mouth, immediately followed by an uppercut, palm thrust, or knee to the jaw. Broken teeth will be the likely result. Depending on the ashtray's composition and density, the ashtray itself might shatter, compounding his injuries. This technique is even more effective when carried out as a rapid, two-handed maneuver.

5. If all else fails, throw the ashtray at your attacker. This should only be employed as a last resort for two reasons. First, once you've thrown the ashtray, unless you've incapacitated your target (unlikely), and unless there's another self-defense-worthy object handy, you no longer have a weapon; and second, hit or miss, you may have just armed your attacker with an object he can now employ against you.

BAG OF DOG POOP

Scenario

You're at the local dog park with your four-legged little buddy when you're confronted by an angry and twisted SOB who's taking it personally that your pooch stole and destroyed his pooch's chew toy. Even worse, your offer to pay for a replacement falls on deaf ears and balled fists. He's anxious to prove he's the alpha dog, and you're his bitch.

What do you do?

Tactics

If you only have a bag of dog poop with which to defend yourself, hopefully the canine responsible for the bag's contents can protect you. However, if your furry, four-legged pal is a Yorkie, Chihuahua, or some other breed of purse pooch, your best bet may just be a tactical deployment of Fido's feces, as the following tactics illustrate:

1. First, pat yourself on the back for going green. The paper bags you're using instead of plastic (standard brown lunch bags are ideal for this purpose, and don't require disposal in landfills) won't just save the planet, they might save you.

2. If your dog's stool is normal, it'll be slightly moist and begin saturating the bottom of the bag as soon as it's collected. If your dog's stool *isn't* moist, you'd be wise to consult a veterinarian after reading this entry.

3. Snap the bag forward then back with exactly the same movement you used as a kid when rat-tailing your friends with a towel. If this

is unfamiliar to you, picture tossing a Frisbee without releasing the disc.

4. At the moment of *snap!* the feces should rip through the now-saturated and deteriorated bag, splattering the target.

5. This tactic won't hurt your opponent physically, but psychologically, it should provide you with just enough of a distraction to kick your attacker in the groin, punch him in the throat, or use any other weapon at your disposal.

 ## GREEN BERET GUIDANCE

Spiderman calls it Spidey-sense. Terry calls it the Reptile Brain. It's that primitive bit of wiring that exists deep inside all of us, something telling you to beware. Like when you go somewhere spooky and your hair stands up on the back of your neck. Don't walk down that dark alley. Don't get in that elevator with that strange person. Guys in the Spec Ops community get those sensations all the time—but they override them. It's their job. For example, when Terry is standing in the back of a C-130 cruising at 16,000 feet over hostile territory in the dead of night and the red light flashes and the ramp drops, he knows that it's "go time." That's when his Reptile Brain starts screaming at him to get his big dumb ass back in the cabin. Like he says, though, it's his job, so he ignores the warning. But you shouldn't. Trust your gut. The writing's on the wall—you just have to be smart enough to pay attention to it.

BARRETTE/BOBBY PIN

Scenario

You and a stranger are riding the elevator when suddenly the stranger reaches out and pulls the emergency stop button, effectively trapping you in the stopped car. He turns around and stares at you with crazy in his eyes and malice in his heart.

What do you do?

Tactics

There's no time to search for anything in your purse, and swinging it like a flail in the cramped confines just won't work. Instinctively, your hand flies up to your hair where you find your barrette. How you use the barrette will greatly depend on its size, type, and composition.

If the barrette is small and thin, like a bobby pin:

1. Clench the bobby pin in the fist of your dominant hand and use your thumb to apply additional downward force. Don't allow more than half of the barrette to protrude; you don't want to risk losing it or breaking it upon contact with your foe.

2. A straightforward jabbing motion is the most effective option; use short, fast strikes—boxers call them rabbit punches—and aim for the eyes, throat, side of the neck just below the ear, or the soft spot just behind the earlobe.

3. A slashing maneuver can also be attempted if you miss your jab strike and have left your arm extended. Simply whip your arm

from side to side as if you were holding a tennis racket, looking to make contact with the barrette's point.

4. At worst, use this tactic as a distraction to grab a more potent weapon, or deliver a strike with your hands or feet.

If the barrette is bigger than your hand:

1. Close your fist over the barrette, allowing each end to extend beyond your fist. You can strike your attacker with the bottom end as if you were wielding a hammer, or with the top end as if you had a knife.

2. For hammer-like descending blows, target the top of the head (especially if your enemy is shorter than you), or the hands and arms (aim wherever you see skin). If your foe is wearing sandals or any other type of footwear leaving his feet/toes visible, drop to your knees and drive the pointed end as deep into his flesh as you can.

3. For uppercut strikes, target the armpit, or the soft skin under the chin. Or fake high and attack the groin. Using your attacker's legs as a guide, drive the barrette straight up, being careful not to push your striking hand out too far, or your opponent could clamp his legs on your wrist, pinning it and leaving you helpless.

4. At worst, use this tactic as a distraction to grab a more potent weapon, or deliver a strike with your hands or feet.

BASEBALL CAP

Scenario

It's a sunny day and you're taking a leisurely stroll in the park when a knife-wielding mugger decides *your* wallet should be in *his* pocket. Naturally, hightailing it out of there would be the wisest course of action, but for whatever reason (old football injury, arthritis flare-up, you're wearing high heels) that isn't an option, meaning you're going to have to stand and fight.

What do you do?

Tactics

Fortunately, you left the house wearing a baseball cap, one of the all-time best hide-in-plain-sight self-defense items. Granted, a hat isn't an ideal object if your intent is to do damage, but when employed against a knife, it's one of the best things you can wear to prevent damage from being done to you. So pull your hat off your head and consider the following options:

1. The easiest technique is to use the cap as a *flail*—a handheld weapon consisting of a handle and one or more moving "heads" connected to the handle by a length of cord or chain. Hold it by the bill, squeezing the outer edges together as close to the cap as possible, and swing it as if it were a racquet, using as much wrist as possible to generate force.

2. If your cap has a buckle or clasp adjustment on the back—preferably one made of metal—the extra weight will give your strikes additional oomph and inflict more pain. But don't worry if

the adjuster is made of plastic; if you swing hard, it'll still deliver a nasty blow.

3. Target the attacker's hand holding the knife. Best case scenario, the blow will cause him to drop the weapon. If he doesn't drop it, there is a possibility your cap will get caught on the knife, partially or completely shielding you from its cutting edge. This will allow you to grab it without cutting yourself, and wrestle it from his grasp.

4. Another flail technique involves gripping the cap by the fabric and striking with the bill. The harder and firmer the bill, the more force you can generate. Aim for your foe's knife hand, using vertical strikes.

5. If the bill is dense enough and scores a direct hit on the knife where the blade pierces the bill, you may be able to pull the knife from your attacker's hand, much like Roman gladiators did when using nets against daggers or swords.

6. You can also try the "bullfighter method," where you hold the cap with both hands on either side of the bill. Strike with hacking blows, targeting your opponent's knife hand or the back of his neck.

7. If your attacker attempts a thrust, you could catch the blade with the hat—be sure to pull your body back, away from the cap—effectively trapping the weapon, giving you an opportunity to deliver a kick or knee strike to his knee, groin, or abdomen. Just be careful not to impale yourself on the blade.

 EXPERT ADVICE

To make your cap more self-defense capable, sew a flat weight (lead or metal) into the back, or add a small, sealable pocket and fill it with birdshot, ball bearings, or change. Specialized caps with these improvements, referred to as Sap Caps, can be purchased online or in specialty stores.

BILLFOLD/WALLET

Scenario

You've just taken out your wallet and are about to hand the nice homeless guy on the corner a dollar bill when he pulls a knife from behind his cardboard "Will work for food" sign and demands that you give him the rest of your cash.

What do you do?

Tactics

Since your wallet is already in hand, you might as well put it to good use with the following tactics. Besides, because of your close proximity to the threat, you really don't have time to go for another weapon:

1. Most wallets are bifold—capable of being folded into two parts. Hold tight onto one half of the wallet and slap your assailant with the other half, which will flop as you swing. You'd be surprised how much force you can generate, even if you aren't a robust individual. This is the same technique used for a *sap*—a flat (or reasonably flat) lead-filled leather pouch or leather-covered metal/ lead plank or stave, often 6–9 inches in length, used primarily as an impact weapon for head strikes, with the goal of dazing someone or knocking him unconscious. Aim for your attacker's knife hand, or the knife itself. Your swift reaction to his threat will probably take him by surprise, and there's a good chance you'll dislodge the knife from his hand. Then run away, or, if you're thoroughly pissed off, step on the loose knife to prevent him from picking it up, and kick him in the groin with your other foot; or,

if he bent down to retrieve the knife, aim for his face or neck.

2. With both of your hands on the wallet—one on each of the folding halves—grab the knife's blade as if the wallet were Pac-Man jaws. Once the blade has been covered with the wallet, squeeze and twist, attempting to pull the knife from your attacker's grasp. Even if you're unsuccessful, the wallet will prevent you from being cut.

3. Remove a few bills from the wallet, scrunch them up, and throw them at the man's feet or to his left or right. If he's truly in need of money, the sight of loose bills will likely grab his attention, giving you the break you need to flee the scene.

BILLIARD BALL

Scenario

You're shooting pool at your favorite billiards hall and sink the 8 ball in the corner pocket. Your opponent decides to welsh on the bet and snatches his double sawbuck off the table. Ten dollars is hardly worth fighting over, so you return your cue stick to the rack and start to leave, but the classless jerk blocks your egress with fists balled, ready to throw down. Since he can't beat you at pool, he wants to prove to his buddies that he can beat your ass.

What do you do?

Tactics

Grab a billiard ball. This unexpected weapon is easy to hold, fits most hand sizes, and allows for a relatively natural grasp. And, even if the table's been cleared, the cue ball should still be on the felt, or waiting in the ball return. Once you have your weapon in hand, consider the following options:

1. Use the billiard ball to smash your enemy using a downward blow. With enough force, a billiard ball has more than enough mass and is hard enough to dislocate a shoulder, or break virtually any bone it comes in contact with, including the skull.

2. Use the billiard ball as a *fist filler* (any handheld weapon that adds more power to a barehanded punch simply by filling out your fist) to bolster a punch. Granted, you'll probably break your hand in the process, but this would likely happen even if your hand

were empty, so you might as well get the added benefit of some additional heft. In most ungloved fights, punches that connect with the jaw, forehead, or any other solid, flesh-covered bone result in a broken hand—or, at the very least, one or more broken fingers. The human body simply isn't designed for fighting. Still, if you want a one-punch knockout, a solid uppercut or cross to the jaw with a billiard ball in hand gives you the best possible chance of achieving that.

3. If you're wearing a long-sleeved shirt or jacket, take off that article of clothing, knot the cuff of one sleeve, then drop the billiard ball into the sleeve's open end. You now have a flail that can be used against multiple attackers. The length of the garment's sleeve will determine its range of effectiveness. A sock can also be used for this technique—athletic knee socks are better than dress socks—but taking one off in the midst of an altercation isn't realistic. Instead, carry an extra sock in your pocket.

4. If you have better than average aim, throw the billiard ball at your enemy, aiming for his head. However, this should be a last-gasp tactic, as you're likely chucking away the only thing that will give you the upper hand. Even worse, if you manage to hit your adversary but don't disable him, he now has an effective weapon to employ against you.

BLANKET

Scenario

You're enjoying a picnic in the park when a mugger invites himself to your party. Unfortunately, your basket of foodstuffs isn't the only thing he wants, and your safety is in serious jeopardy.

What do you do?

Tactics

Using a blanket as a weapon will require you to channel your inner Green Beret, for only a true Spec Ops warrior would have the wherewithal to employ a section of fabric against an attacker. But remember, *any* weapon is better than no weapon—especially when you use these tactics to help you out!

1. If your attacker is armed with a knife, use the blanket as a shield by wadding or folding it up. You may not be able to stop the full thrust, but every millimeter of blade you cover is one less that can reach your vital organs. Depending on the blanket's material, you may also be able to ensnare the knife in the fabric and trap it, or pull it away from the wielder.

2. Throwing the blanket over the attacker's head can disorient him, giving you an opportunity to launch the first strike.

3. If the blanket is large enough, once draped over your foe it can be used as a restraint, pinning his arms to his sides. Similarly, you might be able to use it to tangle your opponent's feet and get him on the ground.

4. If the material is light enough, try hitting your attacker with the blanket using a snapping motion similar to a *rat-tail*—a flexible, whip-like weapon comprised of a rolled towel or any reasonably soft and flexible material that is used with a backhand snapping motion. You want to hold one end and fling at your target, snapping the end in your hand back at the moment before contact to intensify the impact. Knot the striking end of the blanket to further increase impact force. You can also place a rock, padlock, or any other small object of weight within the knotted fold to increase the impact force even further.

5. Hold opposite ends or corners of the blanket to use it the way a bullfighter uses his cape. If your attacker is employing a thrusting weapon against you (knife, sword, torch, pitchfork, etc.), extend your arms as far in front of you as possible, creating as much space between the blanket and your body as you can. When your enemy thrusts, quickly step to either side and cross your arms, pulling the fabric tight. This should trap your foe's weapon. If you pivot in the opposite direction without uncrossing your arms, you should create enough torque to tear the weapon from his grasp.

6. If a tactical application isn't in your wheelhouse, stuff the blanket under your shirt or jacket and use it like soft armor. Even against a gun, depending on its caliber and type of ammunition, the blanket could stop the bullet/projectile or, at the very least, lessen the round's penetration.

BOOK OF MATCHES

Scenario

You're out for a walk when a would-be mugger demands cash. You reach into your pocket, but instead of pulling out your money clip, you come out with a book of matches.

What do you do?

Tactics

Any defense you mount with a book of matches will involve fire, so consider the options and be prepared to strike back!

1. Try the single-strike technique—lighting and throwing one match at a time. Maybe you'll get lucky and burn one of your attacker's eyes or, if you're *really* lucky, the match will ignite your foe's clothing. If your attacker has been drinking and spilled some booze on his clothes, getting the fabric to take a spark is not as farfetched as it sounds.

2. Rather than trust your safety to a single match, you're better off lighting the entire book to send a more potent flame downrange. At worst, a more intense flame will provide a better distraction; most people's eyes will follow the arc of the flaming matchbook in the hopes of avoiding it.

3. Lighting one of your own garments on fire might be the best tactic. First remove the garment, then light one corner of the item. When it catches, swing the garment like a flail, and look for an escape route, because sooner or later the entire garment will be engulfed in flames, making it impossible to hold. At that point, if you haven't caused your foe to flee or found a way to safety yourself, you're right back where you started, and this time your opponent probably won't give you time to grab another object with which to defend yourself.

BOTTLE OF HOT SAUCE

Scenario

You're enjoying happy hour at your favorite oyster bar when the drunk guy beside you accuses you of drinking his beer. At first you think he's kidding, but the expletives he hurls your way confirm that he isn't. In an effort to avoid a confrontation, you offer to buy him a new beer. He responds by grabbing you by the throat.

What do you do?

Tactics

Every oyster bar on the planet—not to mention most restaurants and eateries—has bottles of hot sauce within easy reach. This condiment will give you a few self-defense options:

1. The quickest and most effective method is to use the bottle as a thrusting/stabbing/slashing weapon. Grasping it by the neck, smack the bottom against the edge of the bar or table to produce a circular jagged edge. Be careful where you strike the bottle against the bar or table; if you break it off too close to the neck, you'll end up working with a much shorter weapon. Once you have the broken bottle in hand, follow these tips:
   - Straight-arm thrusts are the quickest and won't leave you overly exposed like a slashing attack might—especially if you miss. Aim for the face or neck.
   - Twist the broken bottle upon contact (like using a key to unlock a door) to inflict maximum damage.
   - If your adversary is wearing pants or shorts comprised of any

soft fabric, a strike to the groin will be extremely effective. If he's wearing jeans or jean shorts, don't bother with groin strikes; cutting through denim is difficult.

2. As a last-gasp tactic, unscrew the cap—or slice/break off the neck—and dump as much of the hot sauce into your mouth as possible. *Do not swallow!* When your cheeks have reached their limit, spit the hot sauce in your attacker's face. Unless he has some rare immunity to cayenne pepper (or even hotter pepper, depending on the sauce), this will temporarily blind him, likely causing him to drop any weapon he's holding when his hands instinctively go to his eyes.

3. Immediately run away or dispatch the dirtbag via punch, kick, or any other method you desire—tactics that can be employed whenever your attacker has been temporarily incapacitated.

 GREEN BERET GUIDANCE

Every morning on the African savanna, a lion wakes up and knows it must outrun the slowest gazelle or it will starve to death. Every morning on the African plain, a gazelle wakes up and knows it must outrun the lion or it will be killed and eaten. Either way, when the sun comes up, your ass better be runnin'. Translation: Be alert. Be ready to go. Have your head on a swivel. Trouble can—and will—find you, even when (and especially when) you're not looking for it.

BOUQUET OF FLOWERS

Scenario

You exit the neighborhood florist with a bouquet of fresh flowers for your honey, and a mugger attempts to lay you out on a bed of roses.

What do you do?

Tactics

There's safety in numbers. In this case, the number of stems in your bouquet, squeezed together tightly, can create a rather potent weapon. So use the following tactics to make sure your attacker wakes up, smells the roses, and gets out of your face:

1. Fresh flowers will have firm stems. Grab all the stems in one hand, squeezing them together as tightly as possible, and stab your enemy with the stem ends, using descending blows. Channel the shower scene from *Psycho*. Some florists encase the bottoms of individual flower stems in plastic tubes with pointed bases. If your florist uses these vials, the plastic points will enhance the impact and, in all likelihood, the damage.

2. Try the previous tactic, only double-handed by dividing the bouquet into two equal bunches. From a strength of impact standpoint you'll need at least five flowers—five stems—in each fist (if dividing the bouquet will result in less than five flowers/stems per hand, *don't* break up the bouquet). For this technique, target both eyes or ears simultaneously.

3. Jam single flower stems up the nostrils of your attacker. The stems of flowers used in most bouquets are more than long enough to reach the brain. And because the brain is rather soft, poking (or puncturing) it with a flower stem will cause serious damage or even death.

4. If the flowers are roses, tear off the plastic wrapping surrounding the bouquet. Hold the stems horizontally with both hands, and, keeping as much distance between your hands as possible, smash the stems lengthwise against your opponent's face or neck. Upon impact, rake the stems left or right so the thorns catch and tear flesh.

5. Instead of using the flowers to attack, you could also attempt to create a distraction by tearing off a handful of flower petals and throwing them in the face of your attacker. If this works, you could quickly follow up with a stem attack without having to jettison the flowers.

6. Depending on the type(s) of flowers and the length, strength, and flexibility of the stems, you could also use the bouquet to bind a subdued attacker's ankles and wrists with the stems.

BOWLING BALL

Scenario

You're having a fun time with family at the local bowling alley when the day takes a frightening turn. A police chase ends in the bowling alley parking lot, and the bad guy races into the building, locks and barricades the doors, and takes all the bowlers hostage—your family included.

What do you do?

Tactics

Although bowling balls are not the easiest objects to manipulate because of their size and weight, they can still be a lifesaver in a pinch. So if a bowling ball is what you have on hand, keep these tactics in mind:

1. Find a bowling ball with holes that your fingers fit in comfortably to ensure a secure grip. Look for the lightest ball that meets this criterion, as it will be the easiest to manipulate. Once you've found the right ball, hold it in your dominant hand (the hand with which you write or throw), and use an underhand lobbing motion (like a slow uppercut) or an overhand windmill motion to hit your attacker with the ball. Either motion will result in a slow, looping blow that, because of the size and weight of the ball, will still be hard for your enemy to block. It doesn't matter what part of your enemy's body you strike—even the lightest ball will likely cause enough damage to give you the upper hand, or even end the threat entirely.

2. If your enemy is armed with any sort of edged or contact weapon (knife, stun gun, shank, etc.), the ball will make an effective

shield. Bowling balls are also especially good against stun guns and Tasers; electricity does not travel through them.

3. Hold the bowling ball with both hands, and be sure to keep your fingers out of the holes. Hold the ball tight against your chest, then throw it with a shoving motion, medicine ball–style, aiming for your enemy's knees or mid-chest. Even an indirect hit can be effective.

4. Unless your enemy has a ridiculously high pain threshold, using a two-handed drop or slam against a fragile target—fingers or toes—will likely end the threat. At worst, your attacker won't be able to run away or wield a weapon.

5. Combating fleeing miscreants is usually frowned upon by law enforcement. However, depending on the circumstances, you could *prevent* someone from fleeing by launching the ball at his feet just as you would bowl normally. Lead along your target's trajectory, aiming ahead of him, essentially allowing him to run into the ball. Time it right and your foe will go down in a heap.

 **EXPERT ADVICE**

Try to land the first strike (pun intended). Survival is not a playground; you won't get sent to the principal's office for hitting first. In a hostage situation—or in any situation where you or a member of your family is being attacked or held against your will—there isn't a district attorney on the planet who would prosecute you for using any means necessary to defend yourself.

BROOM/MOP

Scenario

You're sweeping off your front porch when a would-be home invader makes his intentions clear.

What do you do?

Tactics

No need to look for a weapon. The object in hand will more than suffice. As you engage your attacker, keep the following tactics in mind:

If the broom is in one piece:

1. Hold the broom by the handle and swing it like a baseball bat. Aim at the side of the knees or lower, with the intent to sweep the miscreant off his feet rather than deliver a damaging blow. Once your attacker is down, you have a few options. Running into the house, locking the door, and calling the police is probably the wisest course of action. However, if you live out in the sticks and don't think the police will arrive in time to help you, or if you see that your assailant isn't injured enough to stop him, take advantage of his temporary weakness and deliver one or more blows to his head or neck to put him down for the count.

2. Reverse the broom and, holding just above the brush, swing the handle like a baseball bat, aiming for the temples, neck, elbows, wrists, knees, or shins. By holding the broom by the handle instead of the bristles, you'll undoubtedly have a firmer grip, and therefore be able to deliver a more telling blow.

3. Light the brush end on fire and use as a flaming prod.

4. Holding the handle with both hands, attack your enemy from behind. Get the bar under your foe's chin and pull tight against

his neck to restrict the airway. If your opponent is backed against a fence or wall, a similar technique can be employed via frontal attack by pushing the handle against the throat rather than pulling.

5. Use the brush with or without the handle as a shield, especially against a knife attack. The bristles could potentially trap a knife blade, allowing you to take it away from your enemy.

If the broom is broken:

1. To break the broom, unscrew the brush from the handle or, if permanently affixed, stomp on the handle just above the brush, breaking it off from the handle. That will give you a lighter, more manipulative weapon to wield. Then, using the baseball bat method, swing with all your might. This isn't the time for delicate blows. When your life is on the line, you want to make every swing count, for you may not get a second chance. Any contact is good contact.

2. You can also break the brush over your knee at the handle's midpoint, transforming the single object into two lighter, more maneuverable weapons that can be used simultaneously, similar to Filipino fighting sticks (used in eskrima).

3. If the broken handle has a sharp end, use that end to poke or stab. Concentrate your aim on soft targets (face, neck, groin).

4. Use the brushless handle like a bokken (wooden samurai training sword); vertical strikes, generating force by lifting the handle above your head before starting the attack, can be lethal. Famed seventeenth-century swordsman Miyamoto Musashi dispatched more than a few adversaries with a bokken.

5. As with the whole broom, use the brush with or without the handle as a shield, especially against a knife attack. The bristles could potentially trap a knife blade, allowing you to take it away from your enemy.

6. After separating the handle from the brush, if one end is sharp it could be thrown like a spear, but by now you know that throwing away any weapon should only be considered as a last resort.

CANDLE

Scenario

You're preparing for a romantic night with your significant other. You've turned off the lights and have just lit a candle when a home invader, thinking nobody's home, jimmies the downstairs window and climbs in.

What do you do?

Tactics

Although a wax object is typically not as robust as one comprised of wood or metal, it's still better than an empty hand. So keep these tactics in mind as you prepare to defend yourself:

If the candle is unlit:

1. If the candle is cylindrical, hold it like you would a dagger and attack the robber using a stabbing motion; downward stabs will generate far more power than uppercuts simply because of body mechanics and general arm strength. If the candle is robust enough and pointed enough, it could have the same effect as a knife or dagger: breaking skin, reaching a vital organ (or organs), and ending the conflict.

2. If the end of the candle is pointed, you may be able to break skin, in which case vital organs can be targeted—although it's doubtful the wax will be able to get through bone. Instead, aim for soft targets like the throat or, even better, the eyes.

3. Larger, heavier candles with more surface area can be used as bludgeons and will probably remain intact through multiple

impacts. If your candle is hard and dense, any part of the body will suffice. If your candle is softer, focus your attacks on the joints or the base of the skull.

If your candle is lit:

1. A lit candle can be used to set your enemy aflame. Depending on what he's wearing, simply touching his clothing with the flame could set him on fire. Most people don't wear fire-retardant clothes on a daily basis, so just a moment or two of contact might be enough to allow the flame to catch.

2. You can also stab your attacker with a lit candle in the same manner discussed in the previous list, to inflict additional damage. Targeting the face, especially the eyes, nose, ears, lips, or inside the mouth will prove most effective.

 GREEN BERET GUIDANCE

Observe, Orient, Decide, and Act is a decision cycle phrase coined by United States Air Force Colonel John Boyd in the early 1950s during the Korean War, now also applied to business and litigation as well as military strategy. For example, if a mugger comes up behind an elderly woman taking out cash from an ATM, presses a knife against her ribs, and orders her to hand over her cash, the last thing he's expecting is for the prey to become the predator. So when she whips around, smashes her pocketbook into his face, and begins fighting back with everything she's got, the dirtbag's OODA loop is thrown completely out of whack. And when you disrupt your enemy's OODA loop, you seriously screw up his kung fu. This may be enough to send him running off, looking for an easier target—and it'll allow his targeted victim to get home to her family.

CANDY BAR

Scenario

Craving your daily sugar fix, you stop at the local convenience store for a candy bar. But before you can get your first bite of chocolate goodness, a would-be mugger rains on your taste buds' parade.

What do you do?

Tactics

Surprisingly, the candy bar you're holding gives you a few different options as an improvised weapon:

1. If the candy bar is of a thicker variety (more Snickers than Hershey's Bar), any hammer-like bludgeon technique will work. In all likelihood you're only going to get a few strikes before the bar crumbles or breaks, so don't wimp out—put all your might into the blows. If the candy bar has been frozen it will be considerably harder and, hopefully, more durable, giving this tactic a better chance of succeeding.

2. You can also sharpen a frozen candy bar into a stabbing implement along the lines of a shank. To accomplish this, remove the candy bar from its wrapper, position one of its ends over a table on the diagonal, then hit the bar with your hand. The idea is to break off a piece—as cleanly as possible—giving you a point. If you have a knife, you can simply cut or carve one end of the candy bar into a proper point. If you're going somewhere and need a weapon, but fear a metal detector could ferret you out, a frozen,

sharpened candy bar will allow you to ghost right through the security checkpoint. Even better, you can eat the evidence after the dirty deed was done.

3. Frozen or unfrozen, making a fist around the bar will provide you with extra punching impact. This type of *fist filler* (any handheld weapon that adds more power to a barehanded punch simply by filling out your fist) isn't quite as effective as palming a roll of quarters would be (due to the weight and density of the quarters versus a candy bar) but, in a pinch, it would be better than a barehanded attack. However, if the candy bar is melting and soft, avoid this tactic; the result will probably just be a broken hand covered in chocolate goo.

4. If you need to create a distraction, rip off the candy bar wrapper and tear it into shreds. You can then throw the pieces into the air or into the face of your attacker while you run away, knee or kick your assailant in the crotch, or grab another object in the vicinity that could be used as a weapon.

5. If you've pulled the wrapper off the candy bar, follow up by smushing the candy bar into your opponent's face. The smeared chocolate might obscure his vision, giving you time to get away.

CAR ANTENNA

Scenario

You're just about to get into your car in an empty parking lot when a would-be carjacker decides your car should be *his* car. Unfortunately for you, he doesn't want to leave any witnesses to his crime.

What do you do?

Tactics

The car's radio antenna should be your first grab. Its composition and configuration will give you the following ways to protect yourself. Naturally, the antenna must first be removed from the car. In extreme cold environments it may be brittle enough to simply snap off. Break it as close to the base as possible. In warmer climates or for more resilient antennas, bend it back and forth—again, as close to its base as possible—weakening the metal until it snaps. Or, you could simply try unscrewing it.

1. If your car antenna is flimsy and whippy, you can use it like a *flail*—a handheld weapon consisting of a handle and one or more moving "heads" connected to the handle by a length of cord or chain. Striking bare skin is best, but a solid hit to a clothed area of the body will still hurt—potentially enough to chase your attacker off.

2. If the antenna is thicker and more robust (such as the ones usually found on full-size pickup trucks and SUVs) you can wield it more like a *sap*, a flat (or reasonably flat) lead-filled leather pouch or leather-covered metal/lead plank or stave, often 6–9 inches in length, used primarily as an impact weapon for head strikes with

the goal of dazing someone or knocking him unconscious. Keep in mind that the more solid the antenna, the better its chance of breaking upon first contact. So make your first strike count; target the knees or shins to immobilize your attacker, or the wrists or elbows to make him drop any weapon he may be holding.

3. If the antenna is collapsible, extend it as far as possible to create the most distance between yourself and your attacker. But as a general rule, the further the extension, the weaker the sections. Conversely, if collapsed, the antenna will be harder and capable of a more solid impact. You may even be able to use it as a *fist filler* (any handheld weapon that adds more power to a barehanded punch simply by filling out your fist, such as a roll of quarters, small flashlight, collapsible baton, etc.) to strengthen the force of a punch.

4. When the antenna is extended, use it as a poker or prod. Target the larynx or eyes. If your attacker's mouth is open, you can shove it down his throat. Even a nonlethal blow can trigger a gag effect, giving you the opportunity to mount another attack. You can also aim for a nostril, which, while exceedingly difficult, can result in a lethal blow if the antenna is shoved deep enough into the nasal passage.

CAR KEYS

Scenario

Car keys in hand, you're approaching your vehicle in a busy parking lot when a mugger jumps out from between some parked cars and demands your wallet. After handing it over without a fight, you expect him to run off. He doesn't. Instead, the depraved criminal actually tells you he's not leaving any witnesses alive.

What do you do?

Tactics

As he comes at you, you start to panic. You're unarmed against someone who means you serious harm. That's when you remember the car keys that you're holding—and these tactics on how to use them for self-defense:

1. Hold the keys within a closed fist, extending the longest key between any two fingers. Make sure your fist is tight. You want as little key movement as possible, to reduce the chances of injuring yourself; bracing the rear of the keys against the palm of your hand will accomplish that. Strike at soft targets with straight thrusts or punches, ideally the face or abdomen.

2. If your key ring has multiple keys, extend as many keys between your fingers as possible. Again, keep your fist clenched tight.

3. Use the key ring as a *come-along device*—an object that can be used to grab, hook, ensnare, or lasso an enemy and force him to go where you want. To use car keys in this manner, trap your attacker's finger within the key ring and twist. If your attacker

resists, a simple twist or turn of the object produces considerable pain, causing him to comply with your orders. You don't want this to happen to you, though, so be sure to not put your own finger or fingers through the key ring itself.

4. Tie a string or shoelace to the key ring or connect it to your belt (which you've removed from your pants). You now have a *flail* (a handheld weapon consisting of a handle and one or more moving "heads" connected to the handle by a length of cord or chain) with virtually unbreakable jagged contact points.

5. For an instant distraction, throw the keys up in the air. Most people will reflexively divert their attention to track airborne objects in their immediate vicinity. This will give you the opportunity to run or attack first.

6. Use your car as a swap for your life. Toss the keys at his feet, tell him the car is his, and run like hell. If he considers the offer even for a moment, that moment may be all you need to put enough distance between you and your attacker to escape. Don't forget to yell as you run, making as much noise as humanly possible to attract the attention of bystanders and, hopefully, security guards or members of the law-enforcement community that may be in the area.

7. Use one of the keys to pry the hubcap off of a car in the parking lot. Even many of the newer cars use hubcaps; it's a round plastic insert in the wheel's center that covers/protects the lug nuts. Once pried off, the hubcap can be used as either a shield or as a hacking weapon.

CELLPHONE

Scenario

You're on an airplane, waiting to take off. Suddenly, the man seated beside you jumps to his feet screaming extremist rhetoric. If anyone's going to stop this hijacking before it starts, it's you.

What do you do?

Tactics

These days, just about everyone has a cellphone on them at all times. Airline passengers are no different. Just prior to takeoff and immediately upon landing, you will no doubt see phones in people's hands. So even if your phone isn't out or within immediate reach when you're attacked, there should be plenty to choose from—and plenty of time to use the following tactics to defend your life and those of your fellow passengers:

1. Calling for help seems like the most obvious tactic. Unfortunately, unless your cavalry can reach you instantly—which is virtually impossible—this will probably just provide an oral record of what's about to transpire. That said, even if you can't get service, pretending to speak with a 911 operator and describing the would-be attacker could prevent the attack from happening. Be sure to speak loud enough so the miscreant can hear you.

2. Use your phone as a bludgeon or hacking weapon. Using one of the phone's edges will create the hardest impact and, depending on the phone's construction and quality, might just keep it from breaking apart, giving you the opportunity for multiple strikes.

3. If the phone's screen is glass, you can break it, remove a shard, and use it as a weapon. Insert the shard between fingers of a closed fist. You'll probably cut yourself but, assuming you strike a soft target (face, neck, stomach), the damage you inflict should be substantially greater than what you sustain.

4. If your phone has an extremely loud volume setting, you could use any pre-recorded custom sound file or app as a distraction, signal beacon, or even as a deterrent (recorded gunshots, perhaps?). You may even be able to find a digital file with a blaring alarm that can be used against wild animals, feral dogs, or even humans.

5. If you're attacked in a dark environment, you can use a bright light app to temporarily blind and disorient would-be attackers, giving you the opportunity to flee or mount another attack.

 GREEN BERET GUIDANCE

Combat sports like MMA and boxing are just that, sports. They take place in a controlled environment, there are rules involved—no biting, eye gouging, hair pulling, or punches/kicks to the groin—and there's also a referee who makes sure those rules are enforced. None of those niceties apply to a street fight. In a street fight, your life could very well be on the line, and if you don't take it seriously, there's a good chance you won't be going home. So if a situation has devolved to the point that angry looks and/or harsh words have turned to physical confrontation, do *everything* in your power to make sure you're the one who emerges from the conflict still breathing. All you should be concerned with is seeing your family again, and anything you have to do to accomplish that feat is fair game.

CERAMIC PLATE

Scenario

You're at a restaurant, about to dig into your first course, when a robber enters the establishment looking for more than food. Your table's his first stop.

What do you do?

Tactics

When it comes to defensive purposes, flat, round, Frisbee-sized objects tend to inspire a throw-first mentality. But resist the urge to fling your potential inanimate savior away and try these tactics instead:

1. Use your plate as a shield. The larger and heavier the plate, the more of your body you can protect. Even if you're up against a gun, depending on the caliber and the ammo, the plate could very well deflect or even stop a bullet.

2. If the plate is on the smaller side, you can hold it in one hand and block attacks while simultaneously using your other hand to mount an offense, with or without a weapon.

3. By holding the plate with both hands on opposite sides you can use it in a hacking/chopping manner. A blow to the head or base of the neck could easily end the confrontation immediately.

4. Holding the plate like a discus, you can chop or slash your foe with front-to-back or back-to-front movements. Target the face, neck, or knees.

5. If the plate is broken mid-conflict, use the sharpest shard as a dagger, being careful not to cut your hand on the ragged edge or edges. You can use your shirt or any scrap of loose fabric to help give you a better, safer grip.

6. If you find yourself bound, especially by rope, ceramic shards can be used to slice through hemp, nylon, and many other types of cordage. Or, if slicing through the rope proves impossible, you can use a broken shard to create slack and loosen a knot.

7. Broken ceramic shards can also be secured between clenched fingers to upgrade a punch, or tucked into shoelaces to make a kick more injurious.

8. Pressing a plate tightly against someone's face can render him unconscious or even suffocate him.

9. Jam the plate down the front of a man's pants, then knee or kick him in the groin. If enough force is delivered the plate will shatter, driving the shards into the sensitive area, almost guaranteeing the end of the threat. Obviously, this is easier said than done and will require an absolutely "perfect storm" of actions to pull off but, if the opportunity presents itself, this is the ultimate last-resort tactic.

CHAIN

Scenario

You're securing a trailer to your pickup's tow hitch and are about to lock on the safety chain when you witness a mugging in progress. Good Samaritan that you are, you simply can't stand idly by.

What do you do?

Tactics

Chains are in the category of objects that double perfectly as weapons. Any chain will provide you with numerous possibilities, including:

1. By itself or with something attached to one end, chains make ideal flails. Obviously, length and weight will be the determining factors of how effective they are; do not swing the chain faster or in wider arcs than you can properly control.

2. Find the center of the chain and grasp it with both hands, held shoulder width apart, and swing the chain like a *kusari-fundo* (also called a *manriki* or *manrikigusari*)—a Japanese handheld weapon comprised of a length of chain with a weight on each end that will allow you to strike with either end.

3. If you can get behind your foe, use the chain like a *garrote*—a weapon used to choke or strangle (a.k.a. a handheld ligature device) using a length of wire, rope, chain, cord, or some other flexible material. If you double the chain around your arm, keeping it wrapped over your elbow, the shorter length will make it easier to make the chain taut, thereby enabling you to increase the choking force.

4. Holding the chain in that same manner, you can launch a frontal attack. By wrapping it around your enemy's chest or waist, you can pin his arms to his sides. If you drop lower and wrap the chain around the attacker's thighs to knees, you can hobble his movements or flip him by sweeping out his ankles. You can also launch a horizontal strike to the throat and, once the chain has been wrapped around your enemy's neck, duck under the chain without releasing your grip, turn back toward your enemy and simply pull toward you. This will flip your adversary onto his back with the chain firmly secured around his neck.

5. By wrapping the chain around your fist, forearm, shin, or foot, you can significantly increase the impact of a strike. But be forewarned—a punch with a chain-wrapped fist will likely result in a broken hand. The good news is that if you hit your opponent with a solid shot, you probably won't have to throw another punch.

CHOPSTICKS

Scenario

You're at your favorite sushi bar when a customer becomes incensed over his bill. Too much *omakase*! He knows better than to take his anger out on the expertly skilled knife-wielding sushi chef behind the counter, so he focuses his rage on you.

What do you do?

Tactics

Socially acceptable on all seven continents—some world travelers prefer to bring their own pairs with them wherever they go—chopsticks are among the best hide-in-plain-sight weapons you can find. They're even allowed in the main cabin of commercial airplanes. So pick up your chopsticks and consider the following tactics:

1. The obvious tactic is to use either one or both of your chopsticks as daggers. Even a flimsy, cheap, wooden chopstick can be a potent weapon. Stab your attacker with a downward or side-hand strike, targeting the eyes or neck, especially the carotid artery. The femoral artery in the thigh is also a high-value target. To avoid breaking the chopstick, try to keep the utensil as straight as possible upon impact.

2. Use your chopsticks as punching spears. Squeeze the chopsticks between the fingers of a clenched fist, bracing one end of the chopsticks against the palm—preferably the larger or less-pointed end. You can also use a dime, penny, or small button positioned

at the rear of the chopstick to prevent it from digging into your flesh on impact.

3. If you're wearing lace-up shoes or sneakers, or if your footwear has a gap between the sole and the shoe, tuck/jam the chopstick into place and use it to enhance your kicks.

4. If the attack has transitioned from inside the restaurant to outside and you find yourself being chased over soft terrain, you can conceal the chopsticks point-up in a hole or depression, using them like *punji stakes*—a booby trap consisting of sharpened sticks, usually wood or bamboo, embedded in the ground pointed side up, often at the bottom of depressions or holes. Hopefully, your chaser will step or fall in the hole and the chopsticks will pierce the bottoms of his feet, crippling or immobilizing him. If the hole is deep enough, you needn't sharpen the ends. If the hole is shallow, break the chopsticks so they have a fragmented and jagged end or, if you have a knife, quickly slice one side to make a point.

5. Depending on the sushi bar's decor, you may be able to wrap the pair of chopsticks with fishing line or piano wire and use them as a *garrote*—a handheld ligature device. This chopstick garrote can also be used as a tripwire when the wire-wrapped chopsticks are pushed into the ground.

 EXPERT ADVICE

So-called tactical chopsticks made from titanium, steel, carbon fiber, fiberglass, or a host of other materials are available in the retail marketplace. Some have sharpened points or conceal needle-like daggers.

CLIPBOARD

Scenario

You're taking a survey on a busy street, asking passersby questions related to your topic, when a psycho with an opposing view decides your inquisitive nature is a threat to the world and tries to silence you permanently.

What do you do?

Tactics

Most clipboards are relatively the same in terms of shape and size, usually differing only in composition material and color. As such, the following tactics apply to the lot:

1. Use the clipboard as a shield. Ideal against punches, kicks, head-butts, and handheld weapons, clipboards can also prove to be an effective shield against firearms, depending on the caliber of the weapon and type of ammo being used. If possible, hold the clipboard with your weak hand, freeing up your dominant hand to mount an attack. However, if you feel you cannot grasp or control the clipboard well enough with one hand, forget offensive tactics and hold the clipboard with both hands; top and bottom holds will give you a more secure grip than if you grasp the sides.

2. For an offensive effort, use the clipboard to hack, slash, or slice your opponent. Target the soft skin of the face, the neck or larynx, or your enemy's digits; fingers and toes can easily be broken—in

some cases even severed—with a forceful downward blow from the edge of a clipboard.

3. If you can remove the clip, which is usually comprised of metal, the sharp edge can be used to cut or gouge, or you can open the clip and grab hold of your foe's nose, ear, or genitals.

4. If the clipboard is made of fiberglass, you may be able to break it over your knee or with a stomp of your foot, producing a jagged edge that can be used like a dagger.

5. You can also blow the particles from a broken fiberglass clipboard into your foe's eyes, blinding him.

 GREEN BERET GUIDANCE

When a would-be robber entered a convenience store in Independence, MO, pulled a knife, and threatened a man and his twelve-year-old daughter, some of the store's customers sprang into action. One used a heavy champagne bottle like a club while the others grabbed items off the shelves and began pelting the criminal with them. When the aggressor covered up from the attack the customers tackled and subdued him, holding him down until police arrived. In all probability, none of these folks were trained in self-defense and/or combat tactics. And they certainly didn't do any group practice on how to deal with the situation they'd just faced head-on. But that didn't stop them from using what was at their disposal to end the threat and save the day.

COFFEE MUG

Scenario

Breakfast at your favorite coffee shop is usually a great start to your day. Unfortunately, this morning, your coffee and eggs comes with a side of robbery, courtesy of a ski-masked man wielding a gun.

What do you do?

Tactics

Unless you truly believe your life is in jeopardy, nothing in your wallet is worth fighting for. But if your gut instinct is telling you to act, that coffee mug on the counter is a great place to start. Pick up your cup and use the following tactics to defend yourself:

1. Fling the coffee. Hot liquid is more than just a deterrent—it's an effective weapon that can easily turn the tide of battle in your favor. Even someone with an extremely high pain threshold will likely drop a weapon to initially touch the affected area. Target the face or groin.

2. Bolstering the impact of a punch with the mug is another worthwhile tactic. You can hook one or more fingers through the handle but, depending on the mug's construction, there's a good change the handle will break upon impact, potentially breaking your fingers (and quite possibly your hand) in the process. Still, if the blow incapacitates your foe, it's worth it.

3. If the mug is made of metal and has a thin rim, reversing it and slamming it down onto your enemy's hand (if resting on the counter) or foot (especially if he's wearing soft or open-toe shoes/

sandals) can be a game-changer. At best, the mug will completely sever his fingers or toes. At worst, it will break them. Either way, this type of attack will leave him crippled and vulnerable to any kind of follow-up strike.

4. If your opponent has a knife or any other edged weapon, use the mug to temporarily cover the business end of that weapon, and give yourself the opportunity to attack without worry of being cut.

COFFEEPOT

Scenario

You're at work, refilling your coffee mug at the communal pot, when a recently fired former coworker returns, looking to give the boss a piece of his mind, along with an introduction to the weapon in his hand. Problem is, your boss isn't in the office. So the pissed off ex-employee turns his anger on you.

What do you do?

Tactics

More is usually better than less, especially when it comes to tools for self-defense. In this case, the coffeepot is most certainly in the category of "less." Still, when used according to the following tactics, it's a weapon nonetheless, and, as you already know, anything in your hand beats an empty hand every time.

1. Throwing a punch with a coffeepot (best done when empty) is not a tactic to be taken lightly. The damage you'll inflict when the pot breaks (unless it's some sort of impact-resistant fiberglass) can be severe. Glass shards could very easily kill your enemy. However, you are also likely to suffer some damage, along the lines of putting your hand through a window. Hopefully the cuts and abrasions you suffer will pale in comparison to those suffered by your enemy.

2. If you don't want to risk punching your attacker with the coffeepot, swing the pot like a tennis racquet—backhand or forehand—extending your arm as far away from your face/body as possible

to minimize the risk of being hit by shattered glass shards. Try to hit your enemy with the front half of the pot and not the full pot, otherwise your hand might be caught in the glass explosion.

3. Hold the pot by the handle and strike it with a hard object, just enough to break it but not completely shatter it, then use the broken remains still attached to the handle to supplement a punch attack.

4. Using this same technique, a side-to-side slashing attack might prove better than a punch, because the broken pot will not be forced back onto your hand.

5. If all else fails, throwing a coffeepot (full is better than empty) at your attacker is one of the "thrown weapon" exceptions. It will undoubtedly break upon contact, whether it hits or misses, denying your enemy a weapon to use against you. If you decide to fling the pot at your attacker, just remember to remove that plastic insert (splash guard) that most coffeepots have, as it will likely deflect or diminish the intensity of the toss.

COMB (PLASTIC)

Scenario

You're at the bank, waiting to speak with the branch manager, whom you happen to have a crush on. Since you've got a few minutes before your appointment, you go to the restroom to freshen up. In the midst of combing your hair, you hear a commotion outside the door, and the next thing you know an armed, masked man bursts through the door.

What do you do?

Tactics

This is one of those rare times when vanity may have saved your bacon. Grab your comb and use these tactics to save the day:

1. Grip the spine of the comb so the teeth face downward. Strike teeth-first, targeting any exposed skin.

2. Break off some of the teeth and insert them between fingers of a closed fist, turning your hand into a makeshift spiked gauntlet.

3. Remove enough teeth to allow a dagger-like hold on the comb, striking with the exposed pointed end. If the comb doesn't have a handle, repeat this process so both ends are pointed.

4. Use the removed teeth as a particle cloud that can be thrown in your assailant's face.

5. Break the teeth without removing them from the spine to turn the comb into a saw that will be effective against a variety of fabrics and materials.

6. Bend the teeth so they angle out at different directions. Strike to cause an irregular wound pattern that is more difficult to treat.

CORKSCREW

Scenario

You're at a wine bar sampling some flavorful vintages when a rival sommelier bursts in, intent on causing damage and mayhem to the bar and its patrons. You're centered in the crosshairs and it looks like you're going to be the first victim.

What do you do?

Tactics

While not as versatile as a knife, a corkscrew is still perfectly capable of inflicting damage in a self-defense situation. Grab one from behind the bar and try the following tactics:

1. If using one of the small travel corkscrews (a.k.a. a waiter's corkscrew), hold it in your fist with the base (the part you hold and twist) pressed tight against your palm. Allow the corkscrew (the curly part with the pointy tip) to extend beyond your clenched fist between your fingers, as close to the center of your fist as possible for maximum impact and control. Once the corkscrew is firmly secured in your hand, punch or thrust at your attacker, aiming for the eye, neck, liver, groin, or the femoral artery in the thigh. However, even if you miss one of the aforementioned primary targets, jabbing a corkscrew into any part of your enemy's anatomy will certainly slow him down and possibly stop him altogether.

2. If using a larger corkscrew (a.k.a. a wing corkscrew), first try to separate the corkscrew from the main housing—simply unscrewing it might work—then hold in the manner just described. If the corkscrew cannot be removed from the body, draw the arms

toward the top of the corkscrew, extending the corkscrew from the housing, and hold as you would a dagger or knife. Then strike your attacker with as much force as you can muster. Multiple strikes are better than a single strike, so if you can pull the corkscrew out of your enemy's body without difficulty, repeat this tactic over and over until your assailant is either dead or no longer aggressive.

3. If using an automatic corkscrew, or any corkscrew device with a battery, wait for the corkscrew to extend beyond its sheath or housing. Once extended, remove the battery, which will leave the corkscrew exposed. Use it to strike your opponent as described in the previous tactic.

4. No matter which type of corkscrew is used, upon impact, twist your wrist to drive the corkscrew deeper, all the while maintaining forward (or downward) pressure. Because of the corkscrew's design, you maybe be able to penetrate bone easier than you could with a regular knife.

 **EXPERT ADVICE**

When using any corkscrew as an impact weapon, hold it in such a way that you're able to maintain a firm grip. Grip security should take precedence over comfort. Keep in mind that if you're able to injure your attacker, blood may slicken the grip, causing your hand to slide forward, potentially onto the corkscrew.

CRUTCHES

Scenario

A sprained ankle has left you on crutches. You're hobbling down the street when a mugger decides your condition means you're an easy mark.

What do you do?

Tactics

While using crutches usually means you're dealing with an injury, you'll be happy to have them should you find yourself in a sticky situation. Use the following tactics to get a leg up on your attacker:

1. Use the crutches to create a buffer between you and your attacker. Place the padded armrest against your shoulder as you would a rifle and aim the tip at the middle of your attacker's body. Keep it centered there, and he shouldn't be able to bypass the crutch buffer. Having four or more feet of extra distance between yourself and someone who wants to do you harm can prevent injury from most handheld weapons, including swords and machetes.

2. If your attacker tries to go low and crawl, you can attempt to pin him to the ground by pressing on the back of his neck. Concentrate the pressure you apply to the center of your attacker's neck—his spinal column. It's an extremely sensitive and vulnerable area; the discomfort he feels will likely result in his compliance.

3. Use one of the crutches as a prod or poker, and aim for the neck, bridge of the nose, or groin. If your foe turns his head, a hard poke to the temples or ears can disrupt his equilibrium.

4. Swing one of the crutches like a baseball bat. Because of its size, choke up or hold it in whatever manner gives you the most control or allows for you to generate a powerful swing. Don't worry about your form; looks are unimportant. All that matters is the ease with which you can swing the crutch. Or, if you find this type of swing difficult, hold the crutch under your arm like you normally would and swing that arm, bracing the crutch against your armpit for both stability and strength. This hold will generate power from your entire upper body, making your hit more effective. With this hold, targeting the head may prove difficult. Instead, aim for the knees. Solid contact may result in your attacker needing crutches, as well.

5. If your attacker is running at you, you can employ the old pole spear technique, which was used quite effectively against riders on horseback. Brace the armrest against something firm—the ground, a wall, your chest—and when the oncoming attacker is within range, raise the tip of the crutch so your attacker impales himself on it—if you're lucky.

6. Remove the hand rest—unscrew or simply break it out—and use it as a fist filler to strengthen a punch, as you would use a role of quarters.

7. Some crutches use oversized screws to hold the components together. If your crutches use these screws, unscrew one of them and place it within your closed fist, to be used as a punching spike.

 EXPERT ADVICE

To increase a crutch's destructive potential, remove the rubber bulb covering the tip. This will expose the crutch's point (wood or metal), giving you a better chance of inflicting real damage—including the breaking of skin—on your adversary.

CUE STICK

Scenario

A fun time at the billiard hall turns potentially deadly when a brawl erupts, trapping you in the corner. You simply want out, but one of the brawlers decides to include you in the fisticuffs.

What do you do?

Tactics

As we explained earlier in the book, a billiard ball is a perfect object to choose for a self-defense application. However, if no balls are available, by using these tactics, a cue stick will work almost as well:

1. Swing the cue stick like a baseball bat. Hold the thicker end and swing the narrow end. Knees or shins are much easier to hit than the head.

2. Poke or stab your attacker with the pool cue. Soft areas—face, neck, groin—should be your primary targets. If your opponent raises his arms to attack you, a hard jab to the armpit is extremely painful. To further increase the stabbing damage, unscrew or snap off the tip to produce a jagged edge.

3. Use the cue stick like a sword and attack your opponent with vertical strikes, generating force by lifting the cue above your head. Strike hard and fast, returning the cue to a centered position to guard against your enemy's counterstrike.

4. Attack from behind by holding the cue with both hands at shoulder width. Position the cue under your enemy's chin and

pull back and up, tight against his neck, using your chest against his back for leverage, to restrict the airway.

5. If you back your enemy against a wall, try a frontal attack by holding the cue stick as above and pushing it against his larynx.

6. If you're holding a two-piece cue stick, unscrew it to create two lighter, more maneuverable weapons that can be used like *eskrima sticks*, also known as fighting sticks. These are typically made of wood (but can be metal, fiberglass, or thermoplastic) and wielded like batons, almost always with simultaneous or synchronized strikes.

7. As a last resort, you could throw the cue like a spear but, as we've explained, that will mean willfully tossing away your only weapon and potentially arming your enemy.

DIRTY DIAPER

Scenario

You're changing your infant child on a park bench when you realize a mugger has crept up on you. Because of the added weight of your child, running away is not an option.

What do you do?

Tactics

The purpose of a defensive weapon isn't necessarily to kill or maim—it's simply to stop/neutralize a threat or, at worst, create a distraction that will allow you to escape or grab another object to further your defense. The following tactics will help you do just that:

1. Throw the soiled diaper at your opponent. For all but the most committed attackers, this will probably be enough of a distraction to allow a follow-up kick to the groin or a gouge to the eyes/face.

2. If the diaper is filled with fresh excrement, hold the diaper by the fabric or fasteners and fling its contents at the mugger. Once again, only the most committed criminal will forego covering his face.

3. Smush the diaper in your attacker's face. This will either cause him to retch, providing you with an opportunity to escape or, if you can hold it in place, you may be able to restrict his breathing enough to render him unconscious.

4. If you're a woman and your attacker is a would-be rapist, your best bet might be to turn the soiled diaper's contents on yourself.

Wiping fresh urine and/or excrement on your face and body may dissuade even the most committed predator from choosing you as his next victim. With any luck the smell will trigger your gag reflex, causing you to vomit—a highly regarded anti-rape tactic—giving your rapist yet another reason to look elsewhere for his next victim.

5. Depending on the diaper's material, you may be able to light it on fire to add to the distraction or use to signal someone for help. Disposable diapers are supposed to be flame retardant; however, depending on their country of origin that may not be the case. Still, probably best to assume disposables won't take a flame. But cloth diapers will take a flame quite easily. Keep this in mind if the situation warrants it.

6. If you're running from your assailant and you can find any place to hide that has a door, wipe the excrement in the diaper on the door's handle, making sure to leave as much visible as possible. Not only will your attacker think twice about touching it, but the excrement will make it slippery and difficult to manipulate if he does.

 GREEN BERET GUIDANCE

In *The Art of War*, arguably one of the most important and influential books on military strategy and tactics, Chinese strategist, philosopher, and military general Sun Tzu (544–496 B.C.), writes, "The greatest victory is that which requires no battle." Fighting is stupid when it can be avoided. If you can run away from an altercation, do it! That's not wussing out—that's being smart. Don't get hurt or killed because of your ego.

DISH SOAP

Scenario

You're at your kitchen sink doing dishes when you get the spooky feeling you're being watched. You spin around to find a home invader standing just a few feet away.

What do you do?

Tactics

On any other day, dish soap would be used to make your pots and pans sparkle. Today, if you use the following tactics, it's going to save your life:

1. Squirt the dish soap in your attacker's face. It will temporarily blind him if it gets in his eyes. At worst, even if the soap doesn't completely blind him, the thick viscosity will at least obscure his vision.

2. Getting the soap in your attacker's mouth may trigger his gag reflex, creating a distraction during which you can escape or grab a more effective weapon.

3. Squirt the dish soap on the floor around your attacker. This will reduce his traction no matter what types of soles he's wearing, giving you time to escape. Even if he's barefoot, the liquid soap will make his footing challenging, to say the least.

4. The best tactic might just be to smear as much of the liquid soap on your person as possible. The idea is to get yourself so slippery that your attacker cannot grab hold of you. Be careful not to get it on the bottom of your feet or shoes. As we explained in the previous tactic, anything that will reduce your traction with the floor or ground will be counterproductive to your escape.

DISPOSABLE RAZOR

Scenario

You're about to shave in your health club's locker room when a 'roid-raging musclehead decides a fight is exactly what he needs to help quell the adrenaline rush he's experiencing from his workout. Unfortunately, it's only the two of you in the locker room, so you get the honors.

What do you do?

Tactics

While a disposable razor isn't nearly as effective as a samurai sword or a machine gun, if that's all you've got, use it. So grab your razor and try these tactics:

1. Place the razor (blade side down) on the counter and smash it with your fist, or place it on the ground and stomp on it. You'd be wise to cover it with a washcloth or towel before striking it. The goal is to separate the actual razorblade from its plastic housing. Once the razorblade is loose, use a strip of towel, tissues, Band-Aid (many gym bathrooms have a jar of these), or anything else you have on hand to wrap one quarter to one half of the blade—just enough to give yourself something to hold without slicing your finger. Grip the wrapped portion of the blade and use your index finger to stabilize it by pressing firmly against the back (dull side) of the razorblade. You now have a very capable slashing/slicing weapon. Target the eyes, neck, wrists, or, if your attacker is naked, the genitals. Note:

- If aiming for your attacker's wrists, a vertical slice will bleed out much quicker than a horizontal slice.
- Slicing the forehead directly above the eyes will generally produce copious amounts of blood, obscuring your enemy's vision.

2. Don't discount the plastic housing the blade was secured in. By itself, the handle can be used to poke or jab an attacker, even if the point isn't sharp. You don't need as much force as you think to puncture the carotid artery (neck) or femoral artery (thigh).

3. Secure the razorblade, with the edge facing out, in the tip of your shoe to greatly increase the effectiveness of any kicks, especially if you have the ability to do arcing kicks.

 GREEN BERET GUIDANCE

If home invaders crash your castle or if a mugger selects you as his prey, don't just stick your head in the sand and accept your fate. Don't be an easy out. Make a stand. In the words of Daidoji Yuzan, an eighteenth-century samurai/military strategist from Japan's Edo period: "Commit to study acts of bravery and valor; emulate them. Do not cast your life away as a coward. One way or another death will come. Resolve now how you will face it."

DOG LEASH

Scenario

You and your pooch are enjoying an afternoon walk when a mugger jumps out of the bushes, intent on turning you into a crime statistic.

What do you do?

Tactics

Because a mugger chose to attack you even with a dog by your side, it probably means Fido isn't of the guard dog variety. So unclip the leash from your dog's collar and know that it's on you to end the threat by trying out these tactics:

1. Swing the leash like a *flail*—a handheld weapon consisting of a handle and one or more moving "heads" connected to the handle by a length of cord or chain. If you have a retractable leash, you're better off swinging the end with the plastic handle; the handle's bulk and weight will cause more damage upon impact.

2. If the leash is long enough, make a knotted loop and attempt to use the leash like a lasso. This will take some skill (or luck), but if you can get it over your attacker's head, you can snug the leash tight around his neck and choke him. You can also drop it down further and pin his arms to his sides.

3. Use the leash like a bullwhip. The metal clasp on the end will enable you to generate a decent amount of speed, perfect for inflicting damage to the face or any bare skin. In the event that your leash doesn't have a metal clasp, tie a knot at the end to create

a little extra weight, which will enable more speed than an end that's too light. An expertly targeted strike can also damage or even remove an eye from its socket.

4. With your hands double-wrapped, leaving slightly more than your shoulders' width of the leash, use the leash as a *garrote*—a weapon used to choke or strangle (a.k.a. a handheld ligature device) using a length of wire, rope, chain, cord, or some other flexible material. This same technique can be used for a frontal attack: Hold the leash horizontally, then as soon as the leash makes contact with the neck, wrap and twist. You can then choke your attacker or pivot slightly, drop to one knee, and flip him over your shoulder. He'll end up on his back or butt, directly in front of you, and you can choke him as you see fit.

5. If your opponent is armed with any sort of stabbing weapon, you can use the leash as a *come-away device*. With your hands double-wrapped and held shoulder-width apart (just like the garrote), wait for your attacker to make his move. When he thrusts, wrap his arm with the leash and pull tight. Technically, his arm is now yours to do with as you please.

 **EXPERT ADVICE**

Depending on the type of collar your dog is wearing—spiked, for instance—you might want to remove the collar from your dog's neck, leaving it clipped to the leash.

DRINKING STRAW

Scenario

You're enjoying a beverage at 34,000 feet via the plastic straw you brought with you when a terrorist with a straight razor jumps into the aisle of the plane.

What do you do?

Tactics

Courtesy of the problems numerous airlines around the world have experienced, the list of prohibited carry-on items is becoming longer and longer. Fortunately, drinking straws are not on that list, and you can use the following tactics to use one to protect yourself:

1. Remove the straw from your soda and suck out any remaining drops of liquid. Then, holding the straw firmly (not too tight, you don't want to crumple or damage it), cap the end you've just removed from your mouth with your thumb. This will trap air inside the straw, making it rigid—firm enough to pierce a raw, unpeeled potato. When the terrorist is within range, attack as if the straw were an ice pick or dagger, using either a vertical thrust or a side-hand jab. Target soft areas on the face and neck. If you can strike the eye, continue pushing until the straw punctures the brain. The hands and forearms are also viable targets, as is the crook of the arm. Aim for one of the visible veins.

2. If you're drinking an alcoholic beverage instead of a soda, or any drink with a spicy component (such as a Bloody Mary), suck in as

much liquid as your mouth can hold without choking. (Remember to breathe through your nose.) When the terrorist is within range, suck in the biggest breath possible through your nose and blow through the straw forcefully, aiming your spewage for his face, specifically his eyes. Ideally, the alcohol or spicy component of your beverage will blind the bad guy. Worst-case scenario, his vision will be obscured slightly—hopefully just long enough to allow for a more devastating attack, either by hand, foot, or with another object-turned-weapon.

3. Any liquor that hasn't been diluted with water, soda, or juice can be used to create a makeshift flamethrower holding a flame (match, lighter) in front of the straw when you blow that spirit through.

4. If you still have the straw's paper wrapper, tear off small pieces and place them into your mouth, working them into spitballs. When the terrorist isn't looking, spit them at the back of his neck or, better yet, try to bounce them off the ceiling above him. You're simply trying to create a distraction, to get him looking in any direction other than the one that a defensive effort will come from. Hopefully the other passengers will understand your ploy and join in the effort. Improve this tactic by:

   • Stick a small wad of wet paper on one end of a toothpick to create a tailpiece, providing a greater surface area to catch your burst of air.
   • Insert the homemade dart into the end of the straw closest to your mouth—point facing away—then aim and blow. You can also use the pin from a safety pin, or a straight piece of metal from a paper clip.
   • Target any uncovered skin, especially the face. Keep in mind, this tactic can act as either a diversion, or, if your accuracy is good enough to hit your enemy's eye, a legitimate defensive strike.

DUCT TAPE/ ELECTRICAL TAPE

Scenario

You're in your backyard using duct tape to temporarily mend a fencepost when you realize you're a little too late—an intruder has already gained access to your property and is now standing directly behind you.

What do you do?

Tactics

They say duct tape can be used for anything. Hopefully, you can prove "anything" includes these self-defense scenarios:

1. Grip the duct tape roll like you would the handle of a coffee mug and strike with the outer edge. The tape roll will protect your hand, especially for repeated strikes.

2. If your enemy has a knife or any other edged weapon, wrap some of the tape around your palms. Give yourself a few layers, but don't diminish your ability to close your fist or grab. This tactic will protect you if you try to grab the knife, possibly even allowing you to grab the blade. You can also wrap your wrists and forearms, providing you with extra protection against blade attacks. Prison inmates are known for using tape by itself or in conjunction with toilet paper or cardboard prior to engaging in shank fights.

3. A shoulder-width (or longer) double- or triple-wrapped length of tape, held in two hands shoulder-width apart, can be used to trap your enemy's arm when he throws a punch, or any edged weapon he's holding when he attempts a thrust.

4. A shoulder-width (or longer) double- or triple-wrapped length of tape can also be used as a garrote if you can get behind your attacker.

5. If you can immobilize or render your enemy unconscious, the tape can be used to bind your foe.

EXTENSION CORD

Scenario

You're trying to plug in your ornament- and light-covered outdoor Christmas tree but the electric cord won't reach. So you go inside, returning moments later with an extension cord—only to find yourself face to face with a criminal who wants more than the presents under the tree.

What do you do?

Tactics

The length and weight of your extension cord will play an important role in your self-defense methodology, so keep that in mind while considering the following tactics:

1. Swing the cord like a flail, using the pronged "male" end to inflict damage. You can also tie a small- to mid-sized object to the end for added impact. Note that the longer the extension cord, the greater the buffer distance you can create between yourself and your foe. But be careful, this can also work against you. A longer length means more time between complete revolutions, giving your enemy extra time to get inside your defensive perimeter. If the extension cord is too long, consider doubling and intertwining it. In addition to improving your control, you'll create a heavier flail.

2. Hold the cord in the center, with each hand controlling one side. This will allow a variety of techniques—from simultaneous overhead "slaps" to alternating strikes—along the lines of Japanese fighting chains, a.k.a. *manrikigusari*.

3. Extension cords can also make effective garrotes. By shortening the cord's length, you can greatly increase choking force. Wrap the cord around your hands, forearms, or shoulders to achieve the desired length.

4. If your only option is a frontal attack, hold the cord horizontally and aim for your attacker's throat. Cross your hands behind your foe's neck and twist the cord until it's tight against his skin. Too many twists, however, and the excess overlapping won't allow you to create enough force to properly restrict your enemy's air.

5. Make a large loop in the cord by wrapping one end of the cord twice around it, essentially creating a lasso. When thrown with precision, a lasso can be turned into a noose with a quick tug.

6. Wrap the cord around your enemy's chest to pin his arms to his sides, or tie the cord around his legs to restrict or hobble his movements. If the cord is long enough, you can fully hog-tie your enemy, both hands and feet.

 ## GREEN BERET GUIDANCE

Barry Eisler, international thriller writer and creator of the John Rain series, says, "The two most important things to do for self-defense are not to take a martial arts class or get a gun, but to think like the bad guys and know where you're most at risk." If you've dedicated your life to the martial arts, or combat sports, or routinely train with firearms and weaponry, good on you. Noble pursuits, to be sure, and the preparation—while not a guarantee—will certainly serve you well if a confrontation should arise. But the overwhelming majority of folks have no time or desire for so-called warrior training. If this sounds like you, put yourself in the bad guys' shoes. Ask yourself: What would make for a suitable target? Where would I choose to rob or attack someone? How would I go about trying to commit that crime? By looking at the situation through the miscreant's eyes, you should be able to steer well clear of putting yourself in the crosshairs.

EYEGLASSES/ SUNGLASSES

Scenario

A quiet afternoon at the library turns terrifying when a madman decides to prove he's death cult–worthy by committing horrific acts of violence. You're his first intended victim.

What do you do?

Tactics

In any life-or-death situation, "four eyes" are always better than two. So rip those glasses off your face and use the following tactics to defend yourself:

1. Pop the lenses out of the glasses and use the frame—arms folded— like a dagger. You can either break one of the lens sockets before you strike with it to produce a sharper edge, or simply use it whole. Target the throat or side of the neck, especially the carotid artery.

2. With the lenses popped out, grip the frame with your fingers through the lens holes, and strike with the arms extended. Straight jabs and thrusts will minimize breakage, but only if you strike soft targets—such as your foe's eyes or throat—but even that won't guarantee the arms will remain attached.

3. Break off both arms and use them like daggers. One held in each hand will allow for dual or simultaneous attacks. Once again, target soft areas. However, if one end is sharp or can be broken/ filed to produce a sharp edge, you can increase your number of target areas to include the groin, abdomen, and thighs (aiming for the femoral artery).

4. After removing the lenses, depending on the thickness and sharpness/bluntness of their edges, you can use them for slashing attacks. Hold the same way you would a skimming rock, but don't release; use horizontal or diagonal slashes targeting the face, neck, or any exposed skin.

5. Depending on the type of lenses—glass lenses are much easier to break than plastic or polycarbonite—you may be able to break them in a controlled manner to form a pointed edge along the lines of an arrowhead, shank, or scalpel. Based on the length of the point, you can use paper, fabric, or even a plant leaf to create a safe handle. Reaching vital organs with a point or shank formed from eyeglass lenses is probably not realistic, but there are many veins near the surface of the arms and legs, along with two arteries (carotid, femoral) that are accessible. Or you can target the eyes, face, ears, or groin.

6. If there is bright sunlight coming in through the window of the library, or if you manage to get outside and you have any time to work, you may be able to use the lens to focus a concentrated beam of light onto wood, paper (from the pages of a book), or any tinder to make a fire, and then use the fire against your enemy.

FIRE EXTINGUISHER

Scenario

You're walking down the hallway of your office building when a fight between two of your coworkers breaks out. Next thing you know, one of them has a knife and he's swinging for the fences, not caring what he hits. What do you do?

Tactics

Directly in front of you, in a nook behind a glass door, is a fire extinguisher. Grab it and use these tactics to defend yourself:

1. Pull the safety pin and spray your attacker, aiming for his face. Be ready to flee or follow up with another attack, should you successfully obscure his vision.

2. If there's a tile or smooth stone floor, aim the spray of the fire extinguisher at your attacker's feet—or simply at the floor a few feet in front of him. This could cause him to slip, enabling you to flee or mount a secondary attack.

3. Use the fire extinguisher like a battering ram, striking with the bottom of the cylinder. If the extinguisher is full, holding it high enough for a head strike will be difficult. Instead, target your opponent's chest or below, with the groin or knees being the ideal area of attack.

4. Use the cylinder like a bludgeon, targeting your enemy's toes or feet. Smash or break anything below the ankle and your opponent's maneuverability will be severely limited.

5. Some fire extinguishers have small chains attached to the safety pin that can be easily removed. Depending on the thickness and length of the chain, you can use it as a flail, or, if it's on the shorter/lighter side, you can close your fist around it and use to bolster the impact of a punch or *hammerfist* strike, which uses the bottom of a tightly clenched fist swung with the same motion you would use to swing a hammer.

6. Use the safety pin as a shank or *push dagger*—a short-bladed dagger with a T-shaped handle, allowing for the blade to stick out past a clenched fist.

7. Use the fire extinguisher to break the glass door of the nook within which it's contained. Then use that glass as a dagger or slicing weapon. Wrap the end you plan on using as a handle with any available cloth, such as from your shirt.

8. If your glass-breaking tactic produces many small shards, use a handful of the splintered glass as a homemade shotgun blast. Throw the glass shards into the air and then spray with the extinguisher. The spray will propel the glass particles at your attacker, potentially blinding him. Pressurized liquid and/or foam may conceal the particles initially. If your enemy wipes his eyes, he may accidentally blind himself with some of the glass.

9. While not the most reliable tactic, you may be able to use the fire extinguisher as a missile. Aim the bottom of the cylinder at your enemy and strike the valve with a rock, hammer, or any other hard object. Depending on the model and age of the extinguisher, breaking the valve could result in an explosive release of contents, thereby launching the cylinder in the opposite direction. If you try this technique, make sure you're not standing directly behind it.

FLASHLIGHT

Scenario

You're in bed, about to go to sleep, when a noise outside piques your curiosity. You grab your flashlight and go out to investigate, expecting to find a raccoon going through your trash, or the neighbor's dog again. That's when you discover the noise isn't a stray animal, but a home invader intent on gaining access to your home.

What do you do?

Tactics

When it comes to flashlights and self-defense, bigger really is better. But any flashlight can save your bacon when you use these tactics to defend yourself:

1. Use the flashlight as a bludgeon, delivering the blow with whichever end has the most heft. If for some reason your flashlight doesn't have batteries, fill the battery compartment with rocks, dirt, coins, or even water—anything to pack in more weight.

2. Unscrew the lens, exposing the bulb, and use this end as a poker or prod. You may want to break the glass first, giving you a jagged weapon with which to strike.

3. Remove the batteries and, depending on their size, use one or more like you would a *fist filler*—any handheld weapon that adds more power to a barehanded punch simply by filling out your fist.

4. On a dark night or in a darkened room, you can shine the flashlight in your attacker's eyes to temporarily blind or disorient

him. Depending on the strength of the beam, you can remove the lens and use the bulb without any cover.

5. Smashing the bulb but leaving the filament intact will convert a working, battery-filled flashlight into a poor man's stun gun. This will be especially effective if your attacker has braces (aim for the mouth) or is wearing any sort of metal. Depending on the conditions, you may be able to use rain or any other water to your advantage, as water is an excellent conductor of electricity.

6. When held firmly with your thumb over the top of your closed fist or between your fist's fingers, you can use the handle's screw cap as a slashing tool. Confine your attacks to slashing blows; punching with the cap between your fingers will drive it into your hand.

7. Depending on the handle's thickness, remove the batteries from the housing and stomp on it, collapsing the sides to create a more dagger-like weapon, and use it to stab your attacker.

FORK (METAL)

Scenario

Dinner at the diner comes with a side of terror when the chef, who moonlights as a bank robber, learns the cops are on to him courtesy of a statewide APB that flashes across the diner's TV screen. He runs out of the kitchen, locks the door, and informs all the patrons that you are now his hostages, and he has no problem killing any or all of you if his demands aren't met.

What do you do?

Tactics

The cheap metal fork sitting on the table in front of you might not look like much, but in a situation where any armament is good armament, that most basic of eating utensils can still be a surprisingly effective weapon when paired with the following tactics:

1. Use your fork as a stabbing weapon. Hold the fork in the middle of the handle with your thumb pointed toward the tines. This will afford you maximum control and help you keep the fork straight upon impact, especially if it's made of a soft metal like aluminum.

2. Because the fork will most likely not penetrate deeper than the length of the tines, you may want to snap off all but one of them, essentially converting the fork to a shank. If your goal is simply to wound, the fork as it is will be fine. But if you're looking for an instrument of mortality, the single tine (or even just a broken tip) will be more effective, as you can drive it deeper—potentially

reaching vital organs—than any edged weapon with a crossbar or horizontal component.

3. If the fork feels flimsy, increase its strength by doubling it over, leaving the end with the tines slightly longer than the end of the handle. Now you can hold it in a variety of ways without worrying about breaking it upon impact. Even the "elbow" you've created by bending the fork will be capable of breaking skin and producing a wound.

4. Use this same bent "elbow" to target pressure points (the temple, armpit, neck, etc.) and use the fork as a *come-along device*—any object that can be used to grab, hook, ensnare, or lasso an enemy and force him to go where you want—as opposed to a stabbing implement.

5. If escape is your intent and a closed window is the obstacle, the "elbow" can be an effective glass-breaker, taking the brunt of the impact while offering some measure of protection to the hand.

6. You can also bend the fork around your hand, metal across your fist just below the knuckles, allowing you to strike with a metal lead instead of skin and bone.

 GREEN BERET GUIDANCE

Publius Flavius Vegetius Renatus, a fourth-century writer from the later Roman Empire, said, "Si vis pacem, para bellum." (If you want peace, prepare for war.) This doesn't mean you should go out and enroll in every tactical, martial art, combat shooting, and apocalypse-prepper course you can find. It simply means you should resign yourself to the fact that bad things happen to good people, and living in denial about that reality—the "it won't happen to me" mindset—won't serve you or anyone else you care about well. If that realization coaxes you to broaden your knowledge and skill sets about self-defense, so be it. It's always better to have the knowledge and skill and not need it, than to need it and not have it.

FRISBEE

Scenario

A fun game of Frisbee becomes a fight for survival when a knife-wielding madman enters your area of the park. At first you think it's just some crazy prank—a dark humor video for YouTube or Vine—but when the attacker comes closer, stabbing someone en route, you realize this is going to be a fight for your life.

What do you do?

Tactics

Spartans were legendary for using their shields in battle, both defensively and offensively. And while you probably haven't undergone the same warrior training that Spartans did, nor is your "shield" anything close to what a Spartan carried, in a pinch your Frisbee can serve the same purpose:

1. Use your Frisbee as a shield by holding it with both hands on either side—at 3:00 and 9:00, like the numbers on a clock. The goal is to block each strike or thrust with as close to the Frisbee's center as possible. If your attacker has a blunt-force object or is trying to strike you with his hands or feet, the Frisbee's construction—giving it the ability to flex on impact—will help to cushion or completely absorb the blow.

2. Thrust the Frisbee at the knife, essentially meeting the strike. You actually want your assailant's blade to pierce the Frisbee. Once the blade punctures the plastic, twist the Frisbee right or left as

quickly as possible, making at least a 90-degree rotation. Chances are good the blade will be momentarily embedded in the plastic, just long enough that the twist will wrench the knife from his grasp. Depending on your degree of comfort with a knife, you could either remove the knife and use it against your foe, or throw the Frisbee with the knife still embedded, distancing the blade from the attacker.

3. As an offensive weapon, striking with the edge of the Frisbee can be effective against joints or soft, vulnerable targets like the throat, side of the neck (carotid artery), or base of the neck. The bridge of the nose is also a vital area to strike. A follow-up uppercut strike to a broken nose has the potential to drive the broken nasal bone into the brain.

4. Use the underside of the Frisbee to scoop up gravel, dirt, or sand and fling it at your assailant's face, either blinding him or partially obscuring his vision. Hot water, coffee, salt water, or acid can also be scooped and thrown at your enemy.

5. As a last-ditch effort, you could throw the Frisbee at your attacker. A solid technique can be acquired with practice, allowing you to generate enough force with a throw to momentarily distract or even injure your enemy.

FRYING PAN

Scenario

You're cooking a meal when an intruder bursts into your home via the side door leading into your kitchen.

What do you do?

Tactics

In most kitchens, there are numerous objects you could grab to defend yourself. In this case your hand grabbed the handle of the nearest frying pan. Check out these tactics to learn how you can use it to defend yourself:

1. For the first strike, swing with the pan turned sideways. It'll cut through the air with far less resistance than if the pan were upright, giving you the best chance of hitting the intruder before he can mount an offensive against you. Follow-up strikes can be of any type, holding the pan whichever way is most comfortable and allows you to generate maximum force.

2. If your attacker has a weapon and is already mounting a strike against you, swing the pan vertically, leading with the side of the pan. That way, even if you miss, there's a good chance his weapon will be blocked by the pan's circumference.

3. Use the pan like a shield. Forego any offensive tactics for the moment and concentrate solely on defensive measures. Depending on your assailant's weapon, the pan could very well break it. In the event that he's using his hands or feet, striking the metal pan could injure him to the point that another attack from him won't occur.

4. Tear off the handle or break it off with your foot, and use the sharp end of the handle like a dagger.

5. If the handle is robust enough it can be used as a *truncheon*—a baton, bludgeon, or billy club, often carried by a police officer or prison guard—or as a fist filler to fill out your hand for a punch.

6. If the handle comes free with screws attached, you can strike with these as if they were the business end of a *grapnel*—a device with multiple protruding hooks, clamps, or flukes used for grasping, holding, anchoring, or dragging.

7. With or without the handle attached, the pan's edge can be used for hammer blows or hacking strikes; fingers and toes make excellent targets, as does the base of the skull, base of the neck, and the small of the back.

8. Use the pan to scoop and fling a variety of debris and/or substances—dirt and sand, hot water, broken glass, and more.

GARBAGE CAN

Scenario

You finish up your daily chores by taking out the trash. Just as you reach your garbage can, a mugger jumps out of the dark, surprising you.

What do you do?

Tactics

Depending on the type of garbage can you have (loose lid vs. attached lid), there will be a variety of tactics from which to choose:

1. If you have an old-style metal can with a loose lid, the lid can be used as a shield or an offensive weapon. Hold the lid by the handle a few inches away from your body, creating a makeshift buffer zone to absorb any blows.

2. The lid can be used for strikes. Swing horizontally to hit with the edges, aiming for joints, especially the elbows and knees, or use two-handed vertical smashes targeting the top of the head.

3. The can itself can be used as a suit of armor to some degree. You could feasibly place it over your body and, provided you can see the ground, run back to the safety of your house, your car, or even the neighbor's house, relying on the metal walls to protect you against a variety of weapons and strikes.

4. If the can is the type with an attached lid—usually made of rubber or high-density plastic—you could climb inside it and hold the lid down, once again protecting yourself from most blunt-force

object strikes. However, if your attacker is armed with a gun or a knife, you should abandon this tactic—you'll be a sitting duck.

5. Larger, wheeled garbage cans can be used like battering rams. Keep the lid up and open to protect your head and face. Try to stay low, keeping as much of your body behind the garbage can as possible.

6. Even if the lid is attached, chances are it can be easily removed. Rubber or plastic is more forgiving than metal, and will absorb blows better. It can also catch a knife strike; if the blade penetrates the plastic/rubber, twist or spin the lid to pry away the weapon from your assailant.

7. If the can is light and maneuverable enough, you may be able to drop it over your attacker's head, potentially pinning his arms to his sides.

8. If the can is round, flip it onto its side and roll or kick it at your enemy's legs, hopefully knocking him off balance.

9. Finally, don't discount the garbage within the can. Full or half-full garbage bags can be swung with enough force to knock out a foe. If there are glass bottles or anything heavy in the bag and you have time, arrange it so the weighted objects strike your enemy first.

GOLF BAG

Scenario

You're out on the golf course when a crazy greenskeeper decides to take his salary frustrations out on your foursome.

What do you do?

Tactics

If you're playing golf, then it's fair to assume you have a golf bag, either on your back or in a cart. The bag will present a number of options to defend yourself.

Use the golf bag itself:

1. Every golf bag has a strap; the vast majority are detachable, usually with simple carabiner-like clips. Unhook the strap and use the clip end like a flail. You can bend the thinner, movable part of the clip—pulling it down and out of the clip's body—leaving it open to act as a hook or spike.

2. You can also use the strap as a garrote or noose. Wrap the ends around your hands, more than once if the strap is long (you can wrap it around your wrists and forearms for an extra measure of control or exertion), and loop it over your enemy's head and around his neck from behind, then pull tight. Maintain pressure for about thirty seconds after your enemy stops fighting or goes still, just in case he's "playing possum" in the hopes you'll release your hold prematurely, giving him the chance to turn the tables on you.

3. The strap can also be used for a frontal attack. Loop it over your attacker's head and around his neck and pull your adversary toward you, delivering either a headbutt to the nose or a knee to the jaw.

4. Most golf bags have an insert at the top, a divider to separate the clubs. Many of these dividers are easily removed and can be used as a capture shield. If your assailant has a handheld weapon (knife, baton, stun gun), hold the insert with both hands and use it to block or parry his strike or thrust. If the weapon or his hand extends through the divider, twist or push one of your hands forward, pinning either the object or your assailant's hand within the divider, then take advantage of his weakened situation by kicking him in the groin or on the side of the knee, or simply bring the divider down—taking him and his trapped hand/weapon with it—and kick him in the face. Be sure to hold the divider far enough away from your body so as not to be struck by any object extending beyond it.

5. You can also use the divider as a bludgeon. Hold it flat with both hands and strike with the top or bottom of the insert, or turn it on its side and strike with the edges.

Use what's inside your golf bag:

1. If you're on a golf course with a golf bag, there are numerous items within the bag that can be used. The most obvious is a golf club. Drivers and woods will probably be the longest clubs in your bag, although they will likely break upon first contact. Putters are usually the heaviest and will likely cause the most damage. Any part of the body is fair game, but rather than risk a swing and a miss at the head, fake high and then aim for the legs (knees or shins) and put your enemy down.

2. Golf balls can also be used. If you have a bunch, drop them on the ground, grab a low iron (such as a 3, 4, or 5), and swing away, the goal being to hit your attacker. Low line drives are the best shots

to use to accomplish this, hence the low iron. A golf ball can also be rammed down your enemy's throat; it's roughly the perfect size to block the trachea, staunching the flow of air.

3. Pull some golf tees out of your bag and hold a few in your hand, points out. Then make a fist, allowing the tees to stick out between your fingers. While throwing a punch will likely injure your hand, the additional damage to your enemy from the spikes might be worth it. To help keep the tees in place you can don a golf glove, pushing the tees out through the fabric—or the glove's ventilation holes—essentially creating a makeshift spiked gauntlet.

4. Add golf tees to your shoes; you want to place them so they protrude from the toe, the laces, or between the sole and upper layer. Once the tees are in place, kick in such a way that leads with the points of the golf tees, based on how you positioned them in your shoes.

5. A handful of golf tees can also be used as aerial chaff; simply throw them in the air and when your foe adjusts his gaze to follow them, use the distraction to take the offensive.

 GREEN BERET GUIDANCE

Once you commit to any course of action—or once a decision has been made for you, such as if you're attacked—there's no turning back. Think of an untethered rock climber working his way up a sheer cliff. When he reaches the crux of the ascent, if he remains static then his arms will eventually get tired, he'll lose his grip, and he'll plunge to his death. In a fight, even if your plan of action isn't the *best* plan of action, once the fur is flying and you're in the thick of it, the plan itself becomes irrelevant. By invading your space and making his intentions known, the attacker has made your decision for you. There's no time for indecisiveness. Action is required. As my instructor said during my Ranger School days, when things are going bad and you're in charge, "What are you gonna do now, Ranger?"

GUITAR

Scenario

Your weekly jam session turns terrifying when one of the musicians—a rumored meth addict (now confirmed, judging by this outburst)—goes berserk, lashing out at every person in sight. You try to calm him down, but your soothing attempts make him even angrier, and now he wants to hurt you first.

What do you do?

Tactics

That six-string you've been strumming is the key to getting you out of this situation safely. Keep these tactics in mind as you use your Fender for self-defense:

1. Swing for the fences. Hold the guitar by the neck and let your arms and shoulders do the rest. Swing your hips just before the moment of impact, using your dominant leg for additional oomph, just as you would using a baseball bat. And while a head strike will likely put an end to the conflict immediately, a solid hit to the knee, side of the knee, or shin will probably put your foe down. Follow up immediately with an overhead smash; depending on the guitar, you might only have a stump left.

2. Tear the neck off the guitar and use it as a bludgeon. It'll be much lighter and more maneuverable than the entire guitar and, as such, might make a better weapon. If the broken end is sharp or has a jagged edge, use its uneven edges like a dagger or slashing weapon.

3. Guitar strings can be removed and used like garrotes. However, without anything to wrap them around, generating force might result in injury to your hands. Fortunately, you could wrap the ends around pieces of the guitar's neck or around the tuning pegs to protect yourself. Remember, to properly choke someone into unconsciousness, you'll need to generate enough force for at least thirty seconds.

4. Use the body of the guitar, with or without the neck attached, as a shield. If your assailant has a knife or edged weapon, the blade or sharp edge could become embedded in the instrument, depending on the guitar's construction, allowing you to take it away from him (and possibly use it against him).

5. Smashing the guitar (via overhead slam or foot stomp) could provide you with long (and possibly sharp) splinters that can be used as punching/slashing spikes or, if long enough, daggers. You may want to wrap the blunt (or bluntest) end of the spikes with the guitar strap or any loose piece of fabric you can find to give yourself a better/safer grip.

6. Breaking the neck away from the body but leaving it attached via the strings (connected to the bridge) can result in a large flail that will be difficult for your enemy to block. Because it's broken, the part you're swinging won't move with any regularity and could land a telling blow. However, it's likely the guitar will break completely upon first contact, so make your first strike count.

7. Long tuning pegs can be removed from the head and, when secured between fingers, used as punching spikes.

HAIRBRUSH

Scenario

You're in an airport bathroom freshening up after a long flight when a masked intruder bursts out of a stall, intent on robbing you of all your valuables.

What do you do?

Tactics

In most cases, vanity has no upside. This is one of the exceptions. Grab your brush and get ready to defend yourself with the following tactics:

1. Hold the brush as if it were a microphone, and swing with the bristles aimed at your attacker. Any exposed flesh, especially on the face, should be your primary target. Upon impact, twist your hand or wrist with the intention of dragging the bristles across the skin, creating as much additional damage as possible. If you notice any exposed wounds or scabs on your assailant, aim for those.

2. With the same grip, if the brush's handle extends beyond the bottom of your hand, use the point like a bludgeon. Pressure points make ideal targets, as does the collarbone, base of the neck, and tops of the feet.

3. Hold the brush directly behind the bristles and strike as if you were delivering a slap. A solid impact to the temple or ear can disrupt your enemy's equilibrium. If you target the ear, pulling the brush in any direction upon impact will likely cause additional damage and pain, potentially enough to send your would-be

assailant running or distract him enough to allow you to mount another offensive.

4. If your brush has a cushion below the bristles, you may be able to remove it (with the bristles still attached and intact) to create a lighter and more maneuverable hand *grapnel*—a device with multiple protruding hooks, clamps, or flukes used for grasping, holding, anchoring, or dragging. After hooking your attacker's clothing (or skin) with the bristles, pull down with all the force you can muster in an effort to subdue or pin your attacker. Then call for help, or elbow/knee the now-prone attacker in the face/head (repeatedly if necessary) to knock him unconscious.

5. Depending on the type of brush, you may be able to remove the bristles from the cushion individually. If they don't come out easily, try pulling them out with your teeth. Turn your hand into a spiked gauntlet by inserting a few between the fingers of your clenched fist. Even if the points aren't particularly sharp, with some force behind them they can still injure.

6. Hold individual bristles between fingers of your open hand, which allows for painful spiked backhands or palm strikes.

7. If the situation warrants, one or more loose bristles can be concealed within the mouth and used at the appropriate time as either a weapon, when held between clenched teeth (peck at the eye), or as a lock pick.

HAMMER

Scenario

You're in your garage doing a bit of carpentry when an intruder surprises you.

What do you do?

Tactics

Tomahawks have long been used with great success in hand-to-hand combat. Hammers, while not nearly as effective when it comes to cutting, can be used with similar methodology. Try the following tactics to defend yourself:

1. If you're facing one opponent, a strike with either the claw or the face of the hammer will suffice. However, if you're facing multiple attackers, you may want to begin your defense by striking with just the face. A claw strike has the potential of becoming lodged in your enemy and getting stuck, preventing you from engaging the others quickly.

2. Considering most hammers have a decent amount of heft, any part of the body makes a good target. But before you swing, you should first decide whether you want the blow to simply wound your enemy or be mortal. If wounding is your intention, avoid head strikes at all costs, as they could easily kill your adversary. While the skull is strong, hammer blows—especially from someone in the midst of an adrenaline rush (which you most likely will be)—can easily reduce a skull to powder, thereby destroying its contents, the brain.

3. Use the tip of the handle as a bludgeon. Focus particularly on your attacker's fingers and toes, as well as other fragile targets.

4. If the handle becomes dislodged from the hammer's business end, use it to fill out your hand for a punch (like a roll of quarters), or like a baton for jabs to the throat, solar plexus, ribs, and groin.

5. By itself, the handle can also be effective when pressed against pressure points or, if it's heavy enough, as a *sap*—a flat (or reasonably flat) lead-filled leather pouch or leather-covered metal/lead plank or stave, often 6–9 inches in length, used primarily as an impact weapon for head strikes with the goal of dazing someone or knocking him unconscious. When wielding the hammer in this way, be sure to target the back of the head or base of the skull.

6. If you can get behind your adversary, the hammer can be used as a come-along device. Hold the handle with the business end facing down and the claw forward and curling upward, then jam the hammer between your foe's legs and pull up, digging the claw into your foe's groin or the area between his genitals and anus. It doesn't need to break skin to be effective. With the hammer positioned in this manner, you can lead your enemy virtually anywhere you'd like.

 EXPERT ADVICE

While holding the hammer, make sure your grip is tight but comfortable. Too tight a grip will fatigue your fingers, hand, and forearm far more rapidly than it should—a potential problem if you're in a lengthy conflict with one or more assailants.

HANDFUL OF COINS

Scenario

You're walking down the street when someone asks you for money. You reach into your front pocket and come out with a handful of change. Just as you're about to give him the coins, he draws a knife.

What do you do?

Tactics

Being caught unarmed against a knife—or any weapon for that matter—isn't a good situation, but the coins in your hand are worth far more than their intrinsic value. Use these tactics to defend yourself against your attacker:

1. If your would-be attacker is already within arm's reach, make a fist around the coins and throw a punch. You could first pretend to go for your wallet with your other hand, an attempt at a distraction, to give your punch a better chance of succeeding.

2. You can also try to distract your opponent by throwing the coins in the air. This should cause your attacker to avert his gaze, if only for a moment. It's human nature to look at flying objects when they're in your immediate vicinity, even if they cannot harm you upon contact. When your enemy is distracted, kick him in the groin, punch him in the neck, or simply run.

3. Adding your loose change to a sock, plastic bag, balloon, or any other soft, flexible container will transform it into a makeshift sap or flail, which can be used to knock out your adversary with

a jaw or head strike, or injure him with a strike to a primary joint (elbow, knee, shoulder, etc.).

4. If there's an open flame that can be manipulated in any way, such as a candle in a candle holder or an oil lantern, dropping the handful of change into the fire will heat the coins to a degree that contact with them will cause pain. When the coins are sufficiently hot, fling them at your enemy by using the candle holder/lantern as a catapult of sorts. Be mindful not to touch the coins with bare hands. Aim your throw at your adversary's face or any patch of bare skin.

 ## GREEN BERET GUIDANCE

American author Mark Twain said, "It's not the size of the dog in the fight, it's the size of the fight in the dog." Even if you have the most powerful gun, the most massive club, the most bulging muscles, the most training . . . none of those so-called advantages will guarantee victory in a fight. Here's a perfect example: Kamla Devi, a fifty-six-year-old field worker, was carrying water from a canal to her village in India when an adult leopard attacked her. Kamla could have easily given up and died, but instead she fought back. Using only a pair of farm tools and her bravery, Kamla squared off with the menacing cat for a full thirty minutes, sustaining multiple bites, cuts, and fractures in the process, but ultimately killed the beast. Think about that. A fifty-six-year-old woman fought and killed one of nature's fiercest apex predators with antiquated, hand-me-down farm tools, and she survived. How many thugs out there are even close to being as lethal and vicious as a leopard?

HIGH HEELS

Scenario

A fun night at the club turns into a night of terror when an armed maniac arrives on scene.

What do you do?

Tactics

Being dressed to kill has its advantages, and those stiletto heels you're wearing will do a lot more than simply accentuate your legs. Use the following tactics to defend yourself and get out of there alive:

1. Stomp. Toes, feet, and ankles are no match for a solid stomp from a high-heeled shoe.

2. You can always lead with a kick to the groin and follow up with the stomp. By then your attacker might be on the ground bringing his hands, fingers, and his head into play. But be careful; a stomp to the head could easily kill someone.

3. Remove the heels and use them like fighting claws. By holding the shoes directly behind the heels, you'll be able to exert the most force while still maintaining perfect control.

4. Hold the heel in a reverse grip—heel tip facing up or out—and use it like a dagger, ideal for uppercut-type blows. The groin is particularly susceptible to this form of attack.

5. Depending on the weight of the shoe, holding the heel with the shoe right-side up allows you to take on your assailant with

hammer blows. A strong enough blow to the head—temple or base of the skull—can render a man unconscious.

6. Simultaneous blows to the ears or temples, even if they don't knock out your adversary, can seriously disrupt his equilibrium.

7. One of the heels can be broken off a shoe and used to fill out a fist, bolstering a punch, or applied baton-style against joints and pressure points.

ICE SCRAPER

Scenario

You're scraping ice off your windshield one cold winter morning when suddenly you notice a cloud of condensed breath coming from behind you. You spin around, only to discover a would-be mugger standing there.

What do you do?

Tactics

An ice scraper in the hand is worth ten Tasers in the house. Use these tactics to make this unexpected weapon work to your advantage:

1. Take the ice scraper and jab your attacker in the throat. Even if the scraper doesn't cut flesh, the hard-edged blow should end the conflict immediately. Twist the scraper on impact to maximize the chance that the scraper's teeth will rend flesh. In addition, when you aim at the throat, if your assailant ducks or rushes forward, the ice scraper will catch him in the face, possibly the eyes, ruining his day.

2. If you break the business end of the scraper, the broken and presumably jagged handle can also be effective as a stabbing or jabbing weapon. You needn't break your adversary's skin to get the point across.

3. Use the scraper to break up ice particles from your windshield, which can then be thrown in your attacker's face as a distraction, allowing you to get away or find a more effective weapon. It is

possible some of the ice particles will be sharp enough to blind your enemy, even temporarily, giving you even more time to escape or mount an attack against him.

4. If you can break off a larger chunk of ice that has a jagged edge, or if it rained and an icicle formed in your car's wheel well, use those sharp pieces of ice as daggers. But be sure to make your strike count, as they will undoubtedly break upon first impact.

5. If your vehicle has a permanent antenna that's frozen in place, exposure to extreme cold may have made it brittle. Use the scraper to break it off as close to the base possible and use it as a crop, prod, or poke stick as discussed in the Car Antenna entry earlier in the book.

JUMPER CABLES

Scenario

You're a Good Samaritan who has stopped your car on the side of the road to help a stranded motorist. You break out your jumper cables, but, just as you hook them up to your battery, you realize the person in distress is really a carjacker springing a trap.

What do you do?

Tactics

Jumper cables serve a simple purpose: help people out of a jam. With the following tactics, that's exactly what you're going to use them for here, only not in the manner you originally intended:

1. If the clips on one end of the jumper cable are connected to your battery's leads, touching the other clips together will produce sparks. Quick touches, in the direction of your attacker, will launch sparks in his direction—hopefully enough to drive him away.

2. If your assailant is wearing anything that's metal—bracelet, ring, braces, belt buckle, watch—hooking both cables to those metal bits will deliver a shock. It probably won't be enough to electrocute him, but it will still be a jolt nonetheless. However, if he has a bad heart or uses a pacemaker, the shock could be fatal. Naturally, this tactic can only be implemented if the cables are connected to the battery's leads.

3. Yank the cables from the battery and use them as a whip or flail. Don't swing beyond your realm of control, otherwise you leave

yourself open. A shorter length will result in a faster swing and a harder strike. A longer length will give you a greater buffer, but the slower rotational swing speed will make it easier for your assailant to grab the cable.

4. Use the clips as claws. Squeeze the jaws open to reveal the teeth and target exposed flesh or any sensitive area, especially the groin and neck. If your attacker has long, braided, or thick hair, grabbing a large chunk of hair will allow you to control him.

5. Even with the jaws closed, the clips' metal construction can add tremendous impact to a jab or full-strength punch. Hold the clips between the handles, leading with the clenched jaws. Target the ribs or liver.

LAPTOP COMPUTER

Scenario

You're at the local coffeehouse, writing the great American novel on your laptop, when in comes a robber, intent on making off with the register cash and all the patrons' wallets.

What do you do?

Tactics

When it comes to self-defense, technology usually triumphs, so use these tactics to turn your laptop into a formidable weapon:

1. Because of its size, shape, and dimensions, a laptop computer makes a perfect shield. Hold tightly with hands parallel on opposite sides of the computer. Closing the device will provide greater depth protection. Opening the device will protect more bodily surface area. Granted, it's not going to stop a bullet (it might defeat some, but not all), but against handheld weapons and barehanded attacks, your laptop should do the trick.

2. Most laptops make effective impact weapons. They're light enough to be maneuverable, yet just heavy enough to pack a punch on impact. Strike with the flat of the laptop, putting as much surface area as possible on the target. A blow to the knee or elbow can be just as effective as a blow to the head.

3. Striking with the edge of a laptop, while nowhere near thin or sharp enough to be used like a knife or machete, can still be devastating. You don't need to decapitate your adversary to end an altercation. Concentrate your blows to the neck, throat, knees, ankles, elbows, and wrists.

4. The plastic that makes up a laptop's screen can be removed and broken in such a way that it produces a jagged edge, which can then be used like a dagger. To achieve that jagged edge, remove the screen by smashing the laptop on the floor, against the wall, or with any hard object. Position the now-removed screen on a counter or any raised, flat surface so that it partially sticks out on the diagonal. Hold it in place and smash something against it—your foot will do fine—and when it breaks you should have a pointed edge. To protect your hand, wrap a piece of fabric or paper around the end you intend to use as a handle.

5. If your laptop has a removable battery or disc drive, this can be held and used as an impact weapon, or thrown.

6. A disc or DVD from the drive can also be thrown. Be sure to stabilize the disc by holding your index finger against the disc's edge and throw it in whichever Frisbee-throwing manner allows you to generate the most force (usually sidearm, or with a backhanded flinging motion).

 GREEN BERET GUIDANCE

In stressful situations, remaining calm isn't always possible. This holds true whether you're a trained warrior or a couch potato. We all react differently to stress, and until something goes wrong, there's no telling what your individual reaction will be. However, in some situations, losing it may not be a bad thing. There is a saying: "Nobody wants to fight a crazy person." We like to call it Unleashing the Monkey. Chimpanzees are cute to look at and do funny things, but they're crazy strong, crazy unpredictable, and crazy aggressive. Simply put, they're one of the most dangerous animals on earth. So if something goes down and escape is impossible, you want to tap into your inner monkey. Scream, yell, go freakin' berserk. Become that scary monkey. The bully who cornered you? He didn't even expect you to fight back, let alone transform into a raving lunatic ready to gouge out his eyeballs and chew off his nose. Nine times out of ten, just your fearless bravado will end the conflict before it begins. And for that rare tenth time, the monkey will do the rest.

LIGHT BULB

Scenario

You're in the hardware store picking up a pack of light bulbs when a sketchy-looking guy accidentally bumps you as he passes. The impact knocks a gun from beneath his jacket onto the floor. The two of you lock eyes, and that's when you remember his face from a news bulletin about a recent prison escape. Judging by his look, he knows you know who he is, and the fight is on.

What do you do?

Tactics

If you need to find a random object to use as a weapon, a hardware store is a great place to be. And while the light bulbs aren't the best choice, if that's what you've got when trouble finds you, use these tactics to give you an advantage:

1. Hold the light bulb by the cap and break the bulb at the top (as lightly as possible), with the goal of leaving as much of the bulb intact as possible. Then, with your hand encircling the cap, strike your foe with the broken end. Try to make your strike as straight as possible—regardless of the attack angle—because the remainder of the glass will shatter on impact, and any sideways movement will increase your risk of getting cut.

2. If one light bulb is good, two are better. Use the same tactic, but with a bulb in each hand. Try to strike with both bulbs simultaneously. Unless your adversary is a trained fighter, he won't

be able to concentrate on blocking both of your strikes, meaning one hand/bulb will get through his defenses and hurt him.

3. Some bulbs can be easily unscrewed from the filament. You'll know which type you have simply by twisting it. If you have the twist-off variety, remove the glass bulb, leaving just the cap and filament. Holding the cap like you would a *push dagger*—a short-bladed dagger with a T-shaped handle that allows for the blade to stick out past a clenched fist—throw a straight-armed punch aimed at your adversary's face (ideally one of his eyes), mouth, or neck.

4. For best results use the previous tactic, but use two light bulbs (after the bulbs have been unscrewed and removed), again relying on the fact that your opponent may be able to block one of the simultaneous strikes but not both.

 **EXPERT ADVICE**

In this situation, your first instinct might be to throw the light bulb at your attacker. Don't! Barring an absolutely one-in-a-million lucky toss, they're much too light to cause any real damage if you hit your assailant.

LIGHTER

Scenario

Just as you step up to the register at a convenience store, a weapon-wielding miscreant bursts through the door, intent on robbing the joint. After emptying the register, he fixes his sights on you.

What do you do?

Tactics

Every convenience store on the planet has small impulse-buy items on display by the register. Lighters of all shapes and sizes are always among these offerings. Grab one and consider the following options:

1. Use the lighter as a small bludgeon. Grasp tightly, allowing the bottom, nonworking end to protrude slightly beyond your closed fist, and strike with downward blows. Target your attacker's joints and pressure points.

2. If the opportunity presents itself, smash the bridge of the nose or the hinge of the jaw.

3. By reversing the lighter—working end concealed within your fist—with the bottom protruding slightly, use upward thrusts to target the armpits, chin, and groin.

4. Light the flame and allow it to burn long enough to heat up any metal parts. Touching your foe's hand with the hot part of the lighter might burn just enough to make him drop any weapon he's holding, or distract him long enough for you to gain the upper hand.

5. If your attacker is wearing polyester or any other type of flammable clothing, try lighting him on fire.

6. Try lighting something else around you on fire, then use it as a torch or prod.

7. By depressing the lighter's fuel release without sparking a flame, you can fill your closed hand with butane. Then, without moving the lighter away from your closed hand, create a spark by operating the lighter as you normally would and ignite the smallish gas cloud. This should create just enough of a distraction to allow you to mount an attack or procure a more potent weapon. While you will feel some warmth on your hand, there is little risk of being burned.

8. If you're in a hostage situation in the convenience store, jam a rag or any other flammable fabric into the neck of a bottle of liquor (the higher the proof, the better!). Light the fabric on fire to create a Molotov cocktail. Be sure to throw the bottle at your attacker before the flame reaches the fluid. Aim for his waist; it will be harder for him to duck under or jump over, and even if he sidesteps the improvised explosive, a near miss can still be extremely effective.

 GREEN BERET GUIDANCE

Whether it's a much-practiced martial arts *kiai* (pronounced "key-eye") or your garden variety scream or yell, your voice can be a very powerful weapon. A well-timed scream can scare your attacker and scramble his OODA loop, and it can also trigger his alarm bells. Your scream could bring a new problem for the attacker into the equation: assistance. There's also the psychological warfare aspect of a yell. What if you took your screams to "Unleash the Monkey" proportions? Would a miscreant expecting an easy meal really want to deal with a crazy person? During the Golden Age of Piracy, many pirates would commence *vaporing* just prior to attacking a potential prize. They'd yell and scream at the tops of their lungs, bang anything they could get their hands on that would make noise . . . basically unleash aural holy hell, making their soon-to-be-victims think they were Satan's minions. On many occasions, the fleeing vessel would lower its sails and give up without a single cannon or flintlock being fired.

LIPSTICK/LIP BALM

Scenario

You're touching up your lipstick in the bathroom when your purse catches the eye of another woman. But rather than ask where you purchased it, she tries to steal it.

What do you do?

Tactics

Diminutive can still be dangerous if used properly, so grab that lipstick and use these tactics to defend yourself and your property:

1. With the cap in place, tighten your fist around the lipstick leaving just the tip exposed, rising up from the thumb side of your hand. Strike with this part, targeting pressure points such as the side of the neck, the groin, and the throat.

2. With the cap in place, insert the lipstick cap-out between two fingers of a clenched fist, the same way you would hold a *push dagger*—a short-bladed dagger with a T-shaped handle that allows for the blade to stick out past a clenched fist. Strike with the extended end, targeting soft areas. The eyes are especially vulnerable to a depression strike, a hit where you attempt to force an attacker's eyes down into their sockets, in effect blinding him.

3. Hold the lipstick between the fingers of a flat hand, and use the tube to enhance an open-hand (or backhand) slap that targets the face, ideally the nose.

4. Remove the lipstick from its tube, smush it between your fingers into a paste, then try to wipe it in your assailant's eyes. If you miss but get it in your enemy's mouth, the off-putting taste may be enough of a distraction to give you the upper hand.

5. When mixed with certain liquids or chemicals (gasoline, rubbing alcohol, paint remover, citric acid) that may be present, a lipstick smear makes an effective poison delivery system, even through the pores.

6. Embed fragments of glass (or any sharp particles) into the lipstick simply by pressing down on them. Once embedded, use them to slash your attacker, or enhance the strikes in the previous tactics.

7. If there are any long, possibly pointed objects within reach or in your purse (stick, chopstick, knitting needle, etc.), remove the lipstick/lip balm from the tube and replace with the pointed object. Use this to stab your attacker.

 EXPERT ADVICE

While not a defensive tactic, lipsticks and lip balms are ideal for smuggling small objects like microchips. Remove the lipstick from the tube, insert the microchip into the tube, then replace the lipstick. Lipsticks are also perfect tools for leaving messages if you've been abducted. Try to scribble a mark or an entire word in an area that will be visible to many.

 # MIRROR (HANDHELD)

Scenario

You're using a handheld mirror to touch up your hair or makeup when you see a mugger sneaking up behind you.

What do you do?

Tactics

The overall size of the mirror—the housing or frame and the mirror itself—will dictate the full breadth of options, but use the corresponding tactics to escape from your opponent:

1. Hold the mirror by the handle and swing like a racket. If the frame is heavy—like one of those antique sterling silver types—striking with the back or side of the mirror can produce just as much damage (if not more) than striking with the mirror. Don't worry if the mirror breaks; as long as the frame is intact it will still dole out punishment.

2. If the mirror's handle is long enough, hold it at the base as close to the mirror as possible and use the tip as a bludgeon, or as a dagger if it is pointed or sharp enough. Worst-case scenario, if this strike attempt fails, you can follow up with the previous frame/mirror strike.

3. Smash the mirror—don't worry about the seven years of bad luck—and use one of the longer shards as a knife or dagger. To protect your hand, wrap a piece of fabric or paper around the end you plan to use as a handle.

4. Small shards—the smaller the better—make a great particle cloud that can be thrown in your attacker's face or, if small and light enough, blown off your hand into your assailant's eyes. Be sure to suck in a breath *before* you put your mouth near the shards, otherwise you risk inhaling them.

5. If there's a bright light in the vicinity, or if you have a flashlight, you can "bounce" the beam into your attacker's eyes.

6. Mirrors also make excellent signaling devices, ideal for calling in the cavalry. Simply waggle the mirror back and forth in front of any light source (sun, flashlight, headlight, etc.) and hope someone sees it. This technique usually works best for someone on the ground trying to signal someone in the air, like in a plane or helicopter, but can also be used to attract the attention of someone right outside your window or across the street.

7. Mirrors also make great shields against barehanded attacks or handheld weapons. If you're holding a broken mirror, your attacker may ultimately elect not to try striking you for fear of injuring himself on a jagged edge.

8. Broken mirrors are said to cause bad luck. If your attacker is superstitious, breaking the mirror may cause him to leave you alone. On the other hand, he may not care, in which case the broken mirror is simply bad luck for you!

NAIL FILE/ EMERY BOARD

Scenario

Timing is everything. Your decision to file your nails during a coffee break rewards you with a chance to save yourself when a disgruntled ex-employee bursts into the break room, looking to hurt someone.

What do you do?

Tactics

File this one under 'I' for Improvise and use the following tactics to get one over on your attacker:

1. Hold the file like a dagger and target one of the eyes, the soft spot directly behind the ear, the throat immediately below the Adam's apple, or the carotid artery. If the file is pointed, jab it in the webbing between the fingers or in the crook of the arm.

2. Use the file to alter the shape or edge of any other handheld object in the vicinity. If the object is flat and round or square, multiple edges can be sharpened to create a more effective cutting weapon.

3. Snap the file in two and insert the halves between the clenched fingers of a fist to enhance punches, or hold between the thumb and forefinger and slash like you would with a *neck knife*—a small knife or dagger worn around the neck, designed to be used as an emergency backup weapon. Just a slight brush to the eye is all it takes to temporarily or permanently obliterate vision, thanks to the file's coarseness.

4. If the situation takes a turn for the worse and you and your colleagues are taken hostage, the nail file can be used instead of your voice to alert your fellow captives of your plans. Carve your intentions into a desk or wall. Be as discreet as possible. If your attacker spots your message, you're screwed.

5. If it appears you're going to be tied up, hide the nail file up your sleeve, in your sock, or anywhere else you can reach it—even if your hands have been bound. When your captor isn't looking, retrieve the nail file and use it to file open your bonds. It might take a while, but don't give up. If you're not the only captive, work together; it might be easier for you to file someone else's bonds than your own.

 GREEN BERET GUIDANCE

The phrase "Nous defions" means "We defy." This is the motto by which the Special Forces community lives. And in order to defy, there's gonna be some Close Quarters Battle (or CQB) along the way. The three principles of CQB are: Surprise, Speed, and Violence of Action. If you win all three in a fight, it's game over. The fight's yours. If, however, your opponent trumps you in one category, you had damn well better tip the scales in the others. For example, if your enemy knows you're coming, the element of surprise is gone, so you need to hit him fast and hit him so hard his grandma feels it—and keep hitting him until he's bleeding, unconscious, and no longer a threat.

NEWSPAPER

Scenario

You're sitting on a park bench reading a newspaper when a hoodlum tries to make you his latest mark.

What do you do?

Tactics

Although the Internet and eZines allow for the immediate dispensation of news, you can always find a newspaper, no matter what part of the world you're in. Use the following tactics to give your opponent something other than an update on current events:

1. Roll the newspaper tightly, making the ends hard. You now have a lightweight and highly maneuverable club or bludgeon. Avoid knockout shots to the head (he'll be expecting this and ready to block them) and concentrate instead on targeting joints, the neck, the solar plexus, and the groin.

2. If the newspaper is especially thick, divide it into two sections and roll one bludgeon for each hand. Coordinate your strikes, hitting with double taps to the targeted areas or, if you're ambidextrous, try high-low strikes to catch your assailant off-guard.

3. Hold the newspaper open and use it as a shield. Clearly, it won't stop a bullet, but it could easily impede and potentially trap a knife or edged weapon. Depending on the thickness, it could also absorb a punch or kick.

4. An open newspaper can also be used to "hood" your assailant. You could employ a matador technique, goading your enemy into an attack. Sidestep at the last possible moment, drop the newspaper over his head, then hold tight to smother, sweep his legs out from under him with your leg, or knee him in the groin or thigh.

5. If you have a match or lighter, light the rolled newspaper on fire and swing it at your attacker. Most people are instinctively afraid of fire. Just the sight of the lit newspaper might chase him away, even without being struck by it. Just think of Frankenstein's monster and the villagers. Armed with torches, they had the monster running for his life.

OVEN MITT

Scenario

You're cooking in the kitchen. Just as you're about to remove something from the oven, a home invader bursts in.

What do you do?

Tactics

When fights turn serious, the gloves usually come off. However, in this case, you're better off leaving them on. Use these oven glove tactics to keep your kitchen attacker-free:

1. While not nearly as padded as proper boxing or MMA gloves, an oven mitt still affords your hand some protection. This allows for a hard strike—or repeated strikes—against your assailant with a reduced risk of breaking bones in your hand and/or fingers. Hammer strikes (with the bottom of your fist) will afford even greater protection to your hand, versus typical punches.

2. Jam the mitt in your enemy's mouth to restrict breathing. If you can keep your gloved hand in his mouth—with reduced risk of having your fingers bitten off (depending on your foe's jaw strength, they could still be crushed)—and cover his nostrils, you could render him unconscious or even asphyxiate him.

3. If the mitt isn't made of Nomex or some other nonflammable material, light it on fire then punch or slap your assailant. Make your strikes count. It won't be long before the fire burns through the material.

4. Fill the mitt with sand, rocks, full cans, or anything else with heft, and use it as a flail to strike your adversary. A larger mitt will allow more filling, yet still provide enough fabric to grasp. While any heavy object that fits is good, objects with hard exteriors are the best.

5. Turn the mitt into a spiked gauntlet by pushing nails, tacks, pens or pencils, golf tees, jacks, pins or needles, or anything else with a point through the fabric from the inside. Inserting your hand into the mitt should hold the pointed objects in place—at least for the first strike. Packing anything soft between your hand and the inserted objects (cotton balls, socks, wet newspaper, etc.) will provide some protection upon impact.

 EXPERT ADVICE

You can also use the mitt to fling acid or hazardous chemicals at your enemy. Be sure to remove the mitt immediately following your maneuver; chemicals (especially acid) can easily eat through the material. To be quite honest, you probably won't have any hazardous chemicals or flesh-eating acids in your kitchen—or anywhere else in your home, for that matter. That said, remember to be creative when it comes to your self-defense and survival. Think outside the box so you don't end up in one!

PAPER CLIP

Scenario

You're doing paperwork in the office when one of your recently demoted coworkers flies into a rage. Because you were promoted to his old position, he decides to take his anger out on you.

What do you do?

Tactics

While it's true that paper clips are at the extreme small end of the potential weapon scale, keep in mind that it's not the size of the dog in the fight, but the size of the fight in the dog that's important. Use these tactics to make it home in time for dinner:

1. Uncurl the paper clip nearly the entire way, leaving just a small curl to secure between the fingers of a clenched fist or press against the palm of your hand. Because the uncurled paper clip is small and thin, it will be difficult for your assailant to see. A simple jab toward his face could easily perforate his eyeball, ending the altercation, or at least turning it in your favor.

2. Fold over the tip of the uncurled paper clip into a small hook. In a grappling situation, you may be able to latch onto your enemy's nostril, eye socket, lip, earlobe, or any dangling jewelry he may be wearing.

3. If there is any poison (such as any liquid poison used to kill rodents or insects) available, the tip of the paper clip is an excellent toxin delivery system. Even a small scratch will get the poison into

your foe's bloodstream which will, depending on his strength and resilience, severely weaken or kill him in short order.

4. An uncurled paper clip may be used to pick a lock, but the lock will have to be small, such as the kind you'd encounter in handcuffs. Door locks will likely require an additional tool (such as a tension wrench). However, if you're being chased and you can find a room with a locking door, jam the end of the paper clip into the lock before you enter, then break it off, leaving a piece of the paper clip inside, and close the door behind you. Even if your enemy has the key, the lock will be fouled and won't be able to be unlocked traditionally.

PEN/PENCIL

Scenario

You're in a bank, filling out a deposit slip, when you realize the man standing beside you is wearing a disguise: fake nose, eyebrows, teeth—the works. Just as what's going on dawns on you, you see he's about to reach for a gun concealed beneath his shirt.

What do you do?

Tactics

In almost all cases, taking on someone armed with a gun is a big mistake. But if you can beat him to the punch, lives may be saved—yours among them—so use the pen in your hand and the following tactics to stop this bank robber in his tracks:

1. With a little force, that pen in your hand is a fine dagger. Soft tissue is the primary target, but anywhere you can jam it home will work. The webbing between the fingers, the crook of the arm, the side of the neck (carotid artery), the inner thigh (femoral artery), groin, between the ribs, eye . . . wherever you aim, try to go in straight so all your force is delivered.

2. If for some reason the point of the pen is damaged, the blunt end can still do injury, but you'll need to strike a pressure point or delicate area to make your effort successful. A jab into a vein can lead to blood poisoning (from ink or lead), but this outcome will occur long after the altercation is over.

3. Remove the ink cartridge of the pen to leave behind a hollow barrel that can be used as a blowgun with pins or needles. Target the eyes or throat to produce a devastating result.

4. After the cartridge has been removed, you can also use a pen to momentarily hold and fling acid, gasoline, or some other accelerant (which can then be lit), such as the vodka or whiskey a teller keeps in a desk drawer for those post-work cocktails.

5. Secure a pen or pencil beneath the laces of your shoes or sneakers to use as kicking spikes. They will likely break or be dislodged on first contact, so make your strike count. A simple kick to the back of the heel or calf can cripple even the toughest of men.

6. While not the most advisable course of action, if all else fails, a pen can be jammed into the barrel of a pistol or rifle. Upon firing, it may cause the weapon's barrel to explode, injuring the shooter, possibly severely.

PILLOW/PILLOWCASE

Scenario

You're asleep in bed when you waken to an intruder in the bedroom.
What do you do?

Tactics

All those pillow fights you had as a kid may just save your life. Grab your pillow and consider the following tactics as you prepare to defend yourself:

1. Smush the pillow down into the pillowcase, twist the fabric, and swing away. You're not going to knock out or injure your attacker this way, so you're much better off going for the side of the knees or lower legs in an attempt to sweep him off his feet.

2. Pull the pillow from the pillowcase and replace with a phone, lamp, or anything with heft. This will transform the pillowcase into a very effective flail. In the movie *Bad Boys*, Sean Penn's character filled a pillowcase with full soda cans and wreaked havoc on his assailants.

3. The pillow—inside the case or out—can make an effective shield, especially against hand and foot strikes or edged and blunt trauma weapons. Foam will defend better than feathers; if your assailant is using a knife, the foam could be used to trap the blade and take it away from him.

4. Use the empty pillowcase to shroud your attacker's head, like a hockey player pulling his opponent's jersey up and over his face. As

soon as your foe's vision is fouled, light him up with any method of attack you can muster.

5. If you have a feather pillow, ripping it open and swinging it will produce a cloud of feathers that could create enough of a distraction to allow you to take your assailant by surprise.

6. The pillow, foam or feather, can be used to smother your attacker. It's supple enough to conform to his face, blocking all his airways. Apply pressure for at least thirty seconds after your assailant goes limp, just in case he's playing possum.

PING-PONG PADDLE

Scenario

You're playing ping pong at the local rec center when a silly disagreement with your opponent takes a violent turn.

What do you do?

Tactics

They say that in the land of the blind, a one-eyed man is king. The same concept is applicable to self-defense. If your adversary is unarmed, any object you can use as a weapon against him will give you the upper hand. In this case and with the following tactics, that Ping-Pong paddle you're holding is as good as a baseball bat:

1. Holding the paddle in the traditional manner, swing for the side of the head and ears to disrupt equilibrium. A flat strike to the face can also break the nose.

2. By striking with the edge of the paddle, you should be able to cut through the air with more speed, delivering more force. Target the side of the neck, joints, and small bones like fingers, toes, and wrists.

3. Reverse your grip and jab your attacker with the end of the handle. The groin, ribs, and solar plexus are excellent targets.

4. Use the paddle like a shield. Hold it away from your body to allow your hand and wrist to flex upon impact and better absorb the strike. Be proactive against punches, kicks, and edged weapons, meeting your attacker's strikes rather than simply absorbing them.

5. If the paddle has a thin rubber pad, a knife or other edged weapon could become lodged in it. Twist and pull immediately after impact to potentially rip the weapon from your assailant's grasp.

6. Use the paddle as it was intended, hitting flaming objects (like Ping-Pong balls) at your assailant.

PIZZA BOX (WITH PIZZA INSIDE)

Scenario

You've just finished paying the pizza delivery guy for your order. Pizza in hand, you're about to close the door when he pushes his way inside your home, brandishes a weapon, and demands all your cash and valuables.

What do you do?

Tactics

There's no time to find a more suitable weapon. You'll just have to make do with your pizza and these self-defense tactics:

1. Hold the box with your hands on opposite sides, and use a swatting motion aimed directly at the weapon. Swat to the side—right or left, it doesn't matter—to move the weapon off center. Swatting up or down could still result in an injury, regardless of whether the weapon is a knife or gun. If you successfully move the weapon aside, immediately come forward and close the distance, trapping your foe's arm under your arm, against your body, tight to your armpit.

2. If your assailant has a knife, try to impale the blade on the pizza box. The pizza inside will provide extra resistance and, potentially, extra catching power—especially if the blade is serrated.

3. Open the pizza box and, with one hand on the bottom and one hand holding the top open, use the Pac-Man approach (mimicking the jaws of the Pac-Man video game character) to rush your assailant. Upon contact, shift your body to the side, out of harm's way.

4. If the pizza is hot, hold the pizza by the crust and make a fast flinging motion at your assailant, without letting go of the pizza. The hot cheese will slide off, hopefully burning your attacker, giving you the opportunity to turn the tables.

5. Fold the pizza over once or twice and use its doughy thickness as a buffer against any weapon your assailant is holding. This could work perfectly against a knife; the blade will stick into the dough instead of your body and, if an edge is serrated, possibly even catch and get stuck. Additionally, sauce from the pizza could affect his grip on the weapon.

 GREEN BERET GUIDANCE

When decorated Special Forces combat veteran, humanitarian, and survival guru Mykel Hawke takes people into the field for survival instruction, it's inevitable that at least one of his students will be squeamish about doing all that's being asked of him. If he wants to pack it in, Hawke will hand him a pen and a piece of paper and have him compose a letter that says something like "Dear Mom (or "Dear Dad" or "Dear Spouse"), I love you, but I don't love you enough to survive this situation, so I'm gonna lay down and die. Sincerely . . . ." In almost every case the person ends up crumpling the letter into a ball before he finishes writing it and throwing it at Mykel. Then he picks up the sticks and commences making that fire. Hawke's thesis is simple: Think of whom or what you truly care about—whom or what you love—whom or what you would do anything to protect. That's what you're fighting for.

PLASTIC BAG/ GARBAGE BAG

Scenario

You're walking down the street when a mugger decides to make you his victim. You literally have nothing on you to employ against him, but, as luck would have it, there's a plastic bag at your feet.

What do you do?

Tactics

Who'da thunk it? All those times you were in a grocery store bagging your purchases, little did you know you had an effective weapon right at your fingertips. No, not your groceries—the plastic bags holding them! Forget what the environmentalists say; if nothing else is available, a plastic bag could save your life:

1. If your assailant is armed with a knife, wrap the bag around your weak hand—the hand you don't write or throw with—and use that one to deflect the blade, parrying it away with your bag-wrapped hand the way a fencer parries an opponent's thrust. Chances are the blade hasn't been freshly sharpened and you might be able to grab the blade directly.

2. If the bag is large (such as a garbage bag), you may be able to pull it over your assailant's head. Scrunch it up, holding it as wide open as possible, then go for the hooding. If the bag is a solid color, your assailant's vision will be compromised. If the bag is clear, try to pinch it tight and close off his oxygen supply.

3. Place your shoes, cellphone, or anything else with a little bit of heft into the bag, twist the bag a few times, and use it as a flail. Be

careful not to use anything too heavy or sharp that might rip the bag, rendering your only weapon useless.

4. If all else fails, you could try the "crazy person" routine, and begin speaking to the bag as if someone were inside it. If you're convincing, the mugger might leave you alone.

PLUNGER

Scenario

A clogged toilet requires your attention, but when you enter the bathroom, you discover a robber coming through the window.

What do you do?

Tactics

Never mess with a janitor! Janitors—even if they're just janitors in their own bathrooms—have numerous tools at their disposal, all of which have multiple uses. Among that "grab bag" of improvised weapons, the lowly plunger reigns supreme:

1. Hold the plunger by the suction cup and use it like you would a fencing foil. Even a blunt end can produce significant damage to your assailant from a lunging strike.

2. Break off the end of the plunger's handle to create a sharper tip and use lunge strikes.

3. Hold the plunger by the handle and swing it as if it were an axe chopping a tree, targeting the knees and lower legs in an effort to knock your assailant off his feet. Depending on the hardness (or lack thereof) of the plunger's suction cup, head and body strikes might be futile.

4. Remove the suction cup from the plunger and use the handle like a *truncheon*—a baton, bludgeon, or billy club, often carried by a police officer or prison guard.

5. Remove the handle from the plunger and, with your hand/fist inside the suction cup, use as a protective glove when throwing a punch.

6. With the plunger intact, target your enemy's face with the suction cup. Holding it in place over the mouth and nose will eventually suffocate him.

7. Holding the handle, use the suction cup like a launcher to throw anything unsafe to be held—a roll of toilet paper that you've lit on fire, liquid detergent, feces, or any flammable liquid like rubbing alcohol that could be ignited prelaunch.

8. Dip the plunger in a flammable liquid or secure some form of combustible material in the suction cup and use it like a torch. Most people will run away from—not toward—flames for fear of being burned, so just the sight of the torch might send your attacker scurrying.

POCKETBOOK

Scenario

A thug with evil intent chases you into a dead-end alley. Running away is no longer an option.

What do you do?

Tactics

While every woman's pocketbook contains a different assortment of items, the pocketbook itself can also be a potent weapon:

1. Use the pocketbook like a flail and swing for the fences. Be careful not to wrap the strap around your hand or wrist, otherwise your assailant might be able to grab it and pull you to him.

2. Remove the strap and use it like a whip or flail—especially if it has a metal buckle or carabiner-like clip at one/either end.

3. The purse strap can also be used like a garrote (from behind), or a choking strap or neck pull (from in front). If the strap is long enough, it can be quickly converted to a noose.

4. Dump out the pocketbook's contents and, holding it open by both sides, use it to clamshell your assailant's striking hand, or the handheld weapon he's attacking with. Closing the pocketbook around the weapon should enshroud it long enough to allow you to attempt a disarming/disabling move.

5. Throw the pocketbook's contents at your assailant. This can be done en masse, with handfuls (for smaller items, such as change,

lipsticks, etc.), or one at a time (for larger items, such as change purses, cellphones, etc.). Or, holding the pocketbook open, do a flinging maneuver without letting go, effectively sending everything inside at your assailant. Be ready to follow up immediately with a secondary attack while your enemy is distracted.

6. If the pocketbook is large enough you could hood your foe to disorient or smother him.

 EXPERT ADVICE

Assuming your self-defense tactics prevailed, you'd be wise to bind your assailant until the police arrive. In that respect, the purse strap makes an excellent restraint. When binding ankles or wrists, don't just encircle the bones, but wrap between them as well, preventing your prisoner from being able to wriggle out of them.

POKER CHIPS/ CASINO CHIPS

Scenario

You're playing poker in your favorite card room when one of your opponents, whom you've outplayed all night and busted, gets fed up and decides to give you a bad beating that has nothing to do with cards.

What do you do?

Tactics

We all know what Kenny Rogers says about poker, but in this case, neither standing pat nor tossing your cards into the muck will help you. You need to fight back and, when paired with the following tactics, the poker chips you've been playing with will greatly assist you:

1. Grab a handful of chips, close your fist around them, and punch. Chances are you'll break your hand in the process, but the extra heft inside your hand will create a significantly greater impact.

2. If the chips are flimsy enough you may be able to break them, giving yourself a sharp/jagged surface. Hold the chips—jagged edge facing out—between your thumb and forefinger, and slash. Or insert the broken chips—again, jagged edge out—between the fingers of a clenched fist, and punch; or, so as not to injure yourself, use slashing blows.

3. Fill a sock, shirt, bag, or any piece of fabric with the chips and make a flail. You only need a few to create a weapon that will generate enough speed and power to hurt; a stack of twenty chips will be plenty.

4. Throw a stack of chips into the air. When money or anything relating to currency is thrown into the air, most people can't help but follow the "cash cloud" with their eyes. This momentary distraction will hopefully give you all you need to gain the upper hand.

5. Depending on where you're playing poker or gambling, the chips may be flammable. Obviously this depends on the material used to make them. Try lighting them on fire—or dunking them in an alcoholic beverage and igniting them—then kick or fling them at your assailant using your hat or visor as a launcher.

 GREEN BERET GUIDANCE

Think of every horror movie you've ever seen. The soon-to-be victim is running from the deranged, axe-wielding monster and comes to a locked door. He or she pulls out a set of keys, but just can't seem to get the key in the lock. That scenario is based on scientific fact. During times of stress, fine motor skills go away and oversized motor movements are what work. That's why you see big arm swings, big elbows, big knees, etc.

POWDER PUFF

Scenario

You're literally "taking a powder" in a nightclub bathroom when the club's recently fired bouncer-turned-mugger rushes in, intent on stealing your valuables and not leaving any living witnesses behind.

What do you do?

Tactics

A scream—"Fire!" is universally understood—should be your first move. Not only might it stop the would-be attacker in his tracks, but it should also bring help. Then use your powder puff and the following tactics to save your life:

1. Blow the powder in your attacker's face. From temporarily obscuring his vision to making him choke, the particles could have a variety of effects on your assailant. And if he happens to be allergic to whatever you're using, even better.

2. With the compact closed, use the edge as a bludgeon. Target soft areas like the neck or throat.

3. Remove the mirror from inside the compact, break it, and use one of the longer shards like a dagger. Wrap the powder puff around the lower part of the shard to create a makeshift handle, protecting your hand and fingers from being cut.

4. Use the compact's mirror to reflect light into your assailant's eyes, momentarily blinding him, giving you time to make your escape,

grab another more potent weapon, or simply kick him in the groin.

5. Use the powder puff to asphyxiate your assailant. Press and hold the puff against his mouth or nostrils. His first deep breath will cause him to suck particulates into his airway, temporarily interfering with his breathing. Now in distress, he'll be more concerned with his own mortality, giving you the break you need to flee or beat his ass.

 EXPERT ADVICE

Rumor has it that female spies and assassins have used specialized dehydrated poisons, concealed in their compacts, to eliminate their enemies. If you decide to go this route, make sure you have a layer of wax paper or some other impervious buffer separating the toxic powder from your daily use powder. Your secondary powder could also be gunpowder. In this case, a match or lighter is all that's needed to weaponize it against your assailant.

PVC PIPE

Scenario

You're remodeling an old property you bought with the intention of flipping it. One night, after the contractors have gone home, you stop by to check out the progress. No sooner have you entered when you realize you're not alone—a member of the construction crew also stopped by to steal the new appliances you ordered. Since you can identify him, he has no intention of letting you leave the house alive.

What do you do?

Tactics

One of the rooms you're remodeling is the bathroom, and that means PVC pipe. Fortunately, there's a number of pre-cut pipes of various lengths and diameters to choose from. Given the chance, select one that's the same length of a baseball bat, as it will be the easiest to wield.

Just by its size and characteristics, a piece of pipe will have some obvious uses as a weapon. But here are some tactics you might not think about initially:

1. Hold, tape, or staple a rubber band, or anything with a decent amount of elasticity at one of the pipe's open ends, then put a pen/pencil, stick, or anything that could be used as spear shaft inside the PVC pipe. While holding the rubber band or elastic strap against the back end of the improvised spear shaft, pull back the elastic and let it fly. The maneuver you're going for should emulate a poor man's bow and arrow or slingshot. Divers and freedivers around the world use a very simple device called a *Hawaiian sling*

with great success to harvest fish; the weapon you've just created works on exactly the same principle.

2. Stop up one end of the pipe with the most nonporous thing you can find (ceramic tile, chunks of wood, broken glass, rocks, etc.), then fill the pipe with gasoline or any other flammable liquid (paint thinner/turpentine, liquor, kerosene that may have been stored in the house, possibly the garage). Fling the liquid at your enemy, then light it on fire.

3. You can also use the PVC pipe to carry and fling a toxic liquid or acid. Work fast, or the acid may eat through the stopper or the pipe's plastic sidewall.

4. Jam one end of the pipe into your assailant's mouth or other orifice and use as a funnel for anything from toxic liquid to gasoline to fire ants.

 **EXPERT ADVICE**

In the event your attacker chases you from the home, jump in a body of water and use the PVC pipe as a snorkel to evade your assailant.

QUART OF OIL

Scenario

You're purchasing a quart of oil at the local auto parts store when an armed robber bursts in.

What do you do?

Tactics

Sure, an auto parts store will have numerous objects with which you can defend yourself to choose from, but don't discount what's already in your hand:

1. Open the cap or perforate the canister in one or more places, push a length of fabric (sourced from a rag or a swatch of your clothing) through one of the holes to create a fuse, light it, and throw at your assailant, transforming the quart of oil into a Molotov cocktail of sorts.

2. Pour the oil on the ground and light it on fire to create a barrier between you and your attacker.

3. In the event the conflict moves outside, find a place with some slope, gain the high ground, pour the oil—which will run downhill—and light it.

4. Try to hide from your attacker and pour the oil on the ground around a blind corner. When your assailant comes running, he'll slip and (hopefully) fall, giving you the opportunity to flee or mount the offensive.

5. Pour the oil on your attacker and threaten to light it unless he leaves immediately.

6. This one's risky, but it could still work. Pour the oil on yourself, making yourself slippery and impossible to grab/subdue, then escape as soon as possible.

7. Dump some of the oil into your hand and fling it in your assailant's eyes. This will either completely blind him (even if only for a few seconds), or obscure his vision just enough to allow you to escape or find a better weapon to defend yourself with.

GREEN BERET GUIDANCE

Pay attention to the task at hand. Don't lose focus, even if you're in a situation when it appears as if being unfocused won't have any negative effects. Terry found this out the hard way. He says, "I was kickboxing with a South African fighter—a badass with far more skill than me, who outweighed me by a considerable margin. I had just gotten a new cellphone and had it in my gear bag at ringside. When it rang in the middle of the sparring session, I turned to look at it—just as the fighter was unleashing a meaty punch. The punch caught me flush in the face and dumped me onto the canvas, flat on my back. Lucky for me that was just a sparring session and not the real deal—a helpful reminder to always stay engaged and keep my eye on the prize."

REARVIEW MIRROR

Scenario

You're in your car, stopped at a light, when a would-be carjacker jumps into your passenger seat.

What do you do?

Tactics

If you have any advanced driver training, specifically tactical/defensive driver training, use it. But if you don't, use your rearview mirror and the following tactics to deal with this threat:

1. Grab the rearview mirror dead center, and pull back and down with as much force as you can muster, until the mirror pops off in your hand. Immediately use the mirror to chop at the carjacker's face or throat or, if his hands are in the way, aim for the groin. You want to strike with the edge. If you can continue the same motion that you used to pull the mirror free, even better.

2. After pulling off the mirror, smash it on the dashboard with enough force to break it, then hit the carjacker in the face. Upon contact, grind and twist. The idea is to rend flesh. Dragging the broken mirror against exposed skin should cause him to drop any weapon he's holding. Once again, if the jacker's hands prevent a clear path to his face, aim for the hand or arm.

3. If there's an exposed screw (or any sharp edge) on the back of the mirror where it tore free, use this side with the same maneuver explained in the previous tactic.

4. If you are wearing your seat belt, hit your attacker with the mirror while simultaneously stomping your foot on the accelerator, aiming for the closest immovable object or the back of the biggest vehicle. Upon impact, your seat belt should save you, whereas the unseatbelted carjacker will probably become a projectile.

 EXPERT ADVICE

You needn't worry about incapacitating your attacker—although that would be ideal. You simply want to create enough mayhem to cause him to exit your vehicle, or create a momentary distraction to open your own door and get away. Of course, this isn't always doable; you may be wearing a seat belt, or have a pet or loved one in the back seat. If leaving the vehicle isn't possible, repeat the attack.

 # ROLL OF TOILET PAPER

Scenario

You're in a campground restroom. Just as you exit the stall, someone who isn't a happy camper beelines right for you with mayhem in his eyes.

What do you do?

Tactics

Believe it or not, there are worse objects than toilet paper to have on hand when you need a weapon. And, when you use the following tactics, a roll of toilet paper can do far more than just save your butt:

1. Remove the TP roll from the restroom wall, strip a few inches of TP off the roll so the TP hangs loose, and throw the roll at your assailant. This is one of the few objects that we'll actually advise you to throw as an initial tactic. The TP should unroll as it goes, creating a shape like a poor man's Chinese New Year dragon. Other campers in the area will be drawn to this display, giving you the opportunity to make a break for it or mount an offensive with your hands, feet, or some other object.

2. If you have a lighter or matches, light the trailing end of the toilet paper on fire before throwing. Now in addition to a visual distraction you have a fire weapon that, if it strikes your enemy, could set him alight.

3. Insert your index and middle finger into the center of the cardboard tube, crush the TP down, and use it as a makeshift glove when you strike your enemy. The TP will compress enough to still allow

a reasonably solid impact while cushioning your hand, enough to (hopefully) prevent serious damage to your knuckles and/or fingers.

4. Jam the TP roll into your enemy's mouth. The TP should prevent him from being able to bite your fingers hard enough to cause serious damage, yet still allow you to block his main airway.

5. Remove all the toilet paper from the roll, and fold it over and over to create a shank that can break skin. Prison inmates have been known to use TP shanks with brutal effectiveness. Target the body's softest, most vulnerable areas, especially the eyes.

6. If your assailant is armed with a knife or edged weapon, wrap the TP around the hand, wrist, or arm that you intend to use to disarm him. If nothing else, you may be able to minimize the penetration his weapon is able to achieve against you.

 ## GREEN BERET GUIDANCE

During World War II, British soldiers Eric Anthony Sykes and William E. Fairbairn had to teach common grunts to be skilled commandos in a very short period of time. They needed a hand-to-hand combative program that was quick and dirty. Problem was, it didn't exist—so they created their own fighting system. Called *Defendu*, it was grounded in jujitsu and boxing, with the overlying principle of continually taking ground: Keep moving on your enemy without letting up. And as the history books will show, the Allies came out on top.

ROLLING PIN (AMERICAN STYLE)

Scenario

You're doing some late-night baking in your kitchen. Just as you start rolling out dough, a home invader breaks in.

What do you do?

Tactics

Rolling pins—especially American-style rolling pins, which have handles—are among the group of objects that transition perfectly to a weapon. So grab your rolling pin and use the following tactics to get the attacker out of your home and keep yourself safe:

1. Hold the rolling pin by one of the handles and use it to clobber your opponent. If you strike with a heavy rolling pin—something that could be characterized as industrial size or strength—virtually anywhere you strike your adversary will get the job done. A lighter rolling pin, one of those basic home baker's pins, while much easier to swing faster, won't hit with the same impact, so concentrate your strikes on joints, especially the knees and elbows. Of course, a good crack to the neck or temple will certainly get your point across, no matter what type of pin you're using.

2. Hold the rolling pin with both hands, one on either side, and thrust forward, aiming for the neck, jaw, or forehead. If you drop low, you could also target your attacker's shins or kneecaps.

3. Use the points of the handles to jab your attacker, especially the kidneys, liver, or groin. A longer handle will allow a firm grip

while still giving enough clearance beyond your hand to mount a proper strike.

4. Unscrew the handles from the pin and use them as daggers or grapnels. Longer screws are clearly better than shorter screws.

5. Unscrew the handles and use them as a filler to bolster the strength of your fist, as you would a roll of quarters.

6. Some rolling pins have a central insert within the roller that can be removed after you remove the handles. Use this insert like a baton or eskrima/fighting stick, or to jab at soft targets and pressure points.

 GREEN BERET GUIDANCE

If you act like a victim, you've already become one. Playing the "damsel in distress" or the "lamb being led to slaughter" will ultimately end exactly as it sounds: badly. When going anywhere, if you feel eyes on you, instead of averting your eyes and conveying cowardice, return the gaze. Convey the message: "I know your face. I can identify you. I'm not afraid of you." The same rule applies when diving with man-eating sharks, including the supreme apex predators of the ocean, the great white. Look 'em in the eye. Let them know you're watching. Great whites—like most muggers and rapists—are ambush predators. They want an easy meal. But if they see you staring them down, they're far more likely to wait for a less prepared target.

ROPE

Scenario

You're at a marina, tying a boat to a cleat, when a drug trafficker decides your vessel is the perfect craft for smuggling—only he has no intention of buying it from you.

What do you do?

Tactics

Rope is one of those objects for which there are a million uses—quite literally—and a weapon is certainly one of them:

1. Use the rope as a whip. Depending on the length, you may be able to use all of it or, if it's very long, just use a manageable length.

2. Tie a knot or series of knots at one end, or tie something with a bit of heft at one end and use the rope as a flail. You don't need to tie anything on that's too heavy—you just need something with enough heft to generate some additional speed.

3. Use the rope as a lasso, made by passing the *tag end* (the last part) of the rope around the rope's length to create a loop. Repeat this step, then run the tag end inside the coil you've just created and pull it down, parallel to the length of rope. Now swing the lasso in a circular motion above your head to gain speed and, when you're ready, let it fly. If you successfully drop the lasso onto your target's head/ neck, pull the rope tight. A successful toss and the lasso can easily become a noose. Leave the noose in place to hog-tie the miscreant, or manipulate the slipknot to use as a choke collar or leash.

4. If you're in an "evade and escape" situation, a rope can be used to create numerous types of snares—from those that will simply catch your foe to varieties that will disable or kill him. The easiest snare to make is a spring snare. After making a noose or knotted loop in one end of the rope, tie the other end to the top of a sapling or young tree that is at least three times the height of the prey you're attempting to snare. You'll probably need to climb the tree to accomplish this. Once the rope has been secured, pull it down until the tree is bent and cocked. Secure the bent and cocked tree by wrapping the rope around a small branch, or by creating a trigger mechanism with another branch. It should be taut and on the verge of pulling free. The loop/noose should now be lying flat on the ground. Conceal the loop with some plants, grass, and/or dirt. When your prey steps in the loop, the movement will trigger the trap, the tree will snap upright, the noose will tighten, and your prey will be yanked skyward.

5. A rope can be used as a garrote, although the thicker the cordage, the harder it is to use effectively for this purpose.

6. Separate the strands of the rope's tag end, then tie rocks, weights, or anything sharp to them and use it like a cat-o'-nine-tails.

7. Coat or dip the rope in anything flammable and use it as a fuse to ignite a bomb or fire pit, or to simply create a barrier between you and your attacker.

RUBBER BAND

Scenario

You're at work when a commotion in the neighboring cubicle causes you to look over the wall. One of your coworkers, clearly angered by something, is freaking out. He spots you looking at him and decides you'll be his first victim.

What do you do?

Tactics

If the only object on your desk is a rubber band, put it to good use by using the following tactics:

1. Hook the rubber band onto your thumb and pull it back slingshot-style. When your assailant is within range, let it fly. This is one of those situations when closer is better. In reality, you're not going to hurt him with the rubber band, but most people will instinctively duck or, even better, close their eyes when anything—even something rather puny like a rubber band—flies at their face. Use this momentary distraction to flee or take your coworker out with a punch, kick, flying tackle, or some other object-turned-weapon.

2. Use the rubber band to create a slingshot. Simply unfold a paper clip, hook one end in the rubber band, and fire it at your enemy. Depending on the length and thickness of the rubber band, you could generate more than enough force to break skin or, in the event you hit your foe in the eye, blind him. If paper clips aren't available, anything from a coin—dimes and pennies work best—

to pen caps to staples can be fired using the slingshot method. Once again, aim for the face.

3. Use more than one rubber band when creating the slingshot. Double (or triple) the bands on your finger, and make sure the projectiles are as easy to hook onto the bands as possible. The most powerful hunting spear guns make use of multiple bands to propel the spear in the same way a pulled bow string fires an arrow.

4. Break or cut the rubber band, producing a single rubber length. Hold one end between your thumb and index finger, pull back the other end as far as possible without breaking it, and, when your assailant is within range, let it snap forward. Target the eyes, the lips (very painful), or the tip of the nose. While it's doubtful your assailant will be naked, if he is, the groin also makes an excellent target.

SAFETY PIN

Scenario

You're at the dry cleaner, picking up your clothes when a robber bursts in. He sees you as an obstacle to his payday and makes his ill intentions clear.

What do you do?

Tactics

Your hands are empty and you don't have much to work with in terms of self-defense. That's when you spot the safety pin securing the pickup receipt to your clothes . . . .

1. Open the safety pin and bend the pin 180 degrees, until it's pointing straight. Hold the pin between your thumb and index finger and thrust as if the pin were a miniature fencing saber. Soft targets are the best, but the pin will puncture most clothing provided your thrust is straight.

2. Secure the open and straightened pin between the fingers of your clenched fist and use it to accentuate a punch.

3. Open the pin just enough to make a hook and try to hook your assailant's eye, nostril, or earlobe. If he happens to be wearing a dangling earring, this could also be a viable target.

4. With the open pin concealed in your hand, try to get it into your assailant's mouth. Then punch, knee, or kick your foe in the stomach. The idea is to force him to gasp and suck the safety pin into his throat.

5. If you have a callous on your palm, push the safety pin through the dead skin so it stays in place. Leave the point of the pin exposed, angling away from your palm as much as possible. Use that hand to strike at your assailant with an open palm blow and drive the pin as deep as possible, causing your enemy extreme pain or, if you manage to pierce a major vein or artery, significant blood loss, which could lead to unconsciousness or death.

SALAD TONGS

Scenario

You're in the kitchen when a home invader surprises you.

What do you do?

Tactics

Obviously, a large butcher knife would be the ideal object to grab, but if it's out of reach, those salad tongs will do just fine. Use the following tactics to turn your tongs into a formidable weapon of self-defense:

1. Clamp the salad tongs onto the intruder's nose. The instant you squeeze the tongs closed, twist your wrist in the direction you can exert the most power—for most people, this is clockwise—while simultaneously bringing your arm down to about waist level. Unless the intruder has a fake proboscis, he will be unable to do anything except follow your lead, which should put him on his knees or flat on the floor. With the tongs still firmly clamped, finish the intruder off with a knee to the groin or a stomp to the head. Be sure to use your weaker leg so as not to interfere with your dominant hand clutching the tongs.

2. With tongs spread apart as wide as they will go, thrust them at the intruder's throat, aiming just above the Adam's apple. Squeeze the intruder's flesh, twist clockwise, and pull with all your strength, throwing your weight backward to maximize leverage. If done correctly, a chunk of the intruder's neck and trachea will tear free, putting an end to the threat—and the intruder.

3. If the intruder is male and wearing loose shorts or sweatpants, or happens to be naked, you can emulate Tactic #2 but change your point of attack from his throat to his genitals. Squeeze, twist, and pull. If you hear a high-pitched scream, you've done the move correctly.

4. Squeeze the tongs together and use to stab your attacker, just like you would a dagger. Since most tongs have a curved but occasionally sharp edge, a strike with some force behind it will easily break flesh.

5. Pull the tongs apart—breaking the spring if necessary—until they open 180 degrees and are now in a straight line. Hold them with both hands in the center, and use them as a small, double-edged fighting stick.

SALT

Scenario

You're having dinner at your favorite restaurant when the establishment comes under siege by a lone robber.

What do you do?

Tactics

The act of throwing salt over your shoulder for luck has long been used by the superstitious. In this scenario, science trumps belief and, if you follow these tactics, you can actually use the salt to save your life:

1. Take as large a handful of salt as possible and throw it in your assailant's face. Even just one grain of salt in his eye will be enough to obscure his vision. Use that opportunity to grab a more potent weapon with which to dispatch him.

2. Wet your fist with water, saliva, or any liquid in your immediate vicinity, then pour salt over it or dip your hand in the salt. You want to get as many grains to stick as possible so when you strike—punch or slap—the coarseness causes additional damage. Follow-up strikes will force salt into open wounds, increasing the pain your assailant will feel, possibly causing him to run off.

3. Add salt to water, fill your mouth with as much of the salted water as you can hold, and spit it in your assailant's face. Once again, the goal is to blind your opponent—even temporarily—giving you the opportunity to flee or mount a more potent offensive.

SCARF/NECKTIE

Scenario

You're dressed to the nines at your favorite club when an argument between patrons morphs into a multiperson melee. You're caught in the crossfire.

What do you do?

Tactics

Quickly undo that Windsor knot, remove your tie, and use the following tactics to put it to good use:

1. Wrap the tie around both of your hands to create a garrote, and use it to choke your attacker, either from behind or in front.

2. Wrap the tie around both of your hands as in the previous tactic, but instead of choking your opponent, use this length of tie to catch your assailant's hand or foot when he attempts to strike you. Simply cross your hands around his striking limb, pull tight, and then pivot to throw him or drop down to take him down with you. Without releasing your hold on his trapped limb, pull it behind his back to subdue your attacker or break the limb.

3. Knot one end of the tie and use it as a flail. Tying something with heft to the tie or wrapping the tie around something weighty will allow you to generate more speed, and therefore cause more damage. If you have a tiepin or tie tack, reposition it to the end you plan on using as a flail. Exposing the point or sharp end will increase the damage.

4. Wrap the tie around your hand to create a makeshift protective glove. It will cushion the blow of a strike, and will hopefully protect your hand and fingers from breaking, while still allowing for a solid impact.

SCUBA TANK

Scenario

You've just climbed back into the boat after a dive when you realize a pirate has boarded your vessel, and is intent on throwing you overboard.
What do you do?

Tactics

Quickly slip out of your dive harness or BC (buoyancy compensator), remove the scuba tank from its constraints, and use the following tactics to defend your life:

1. Use the scuba tank as a bludgeon either by overhead smash (if you have the strength) or, for the rest of us mortals, try to simply lift and drop onto your attacker's toes.

2. Place the tank on the ground with the valve facing you, and strike the valve with anything metal and heavy, such as a mallet, wrench, or one of those small metal billy clubs that big-game fishermen use for subduing large fish after they've been boated. This action will pop the valve, transforming the scuba tank into a rocket.

3. If you've seen the movie *Jaws*, then you know about a scuba tank's potential explosive power. Duplicate the explosion scene from the movie by finding something to puncture the tank with from afar—bow and arrow, spear gun, slingshot, etc. Just be sure you're far enough away from the tank when it blows, or else you run the risk of being hit by shrapnel.

4. Roll the scuba tank at your assailant's feet. It will either crush his toes, trip him up, or cause him to leap out of the way. When your attacker is airborne, try to take out his legs (with a shoulder or flying tackle) or flee, locking yourself in a secured area of the boat (if there is one).

5. If the tank is made of aluminum, it will float. However, if it is made of steel, it is negatively buoyant. Tie or hook your BC's straps onto your assailant and push him overboard.

6. Jam the regulator into your assailant's mouth or, if you don't have any hoses, force his mouth directly onto the nozzle, open the valve all the way, and rupture your attacker's lungs via overinflation.

 ## GREEN BERET GUIDANCE

One of the famous lines from *Apocalypse Now*, one of the most epic war movies of all time, spoken by Captain Benjamin L. Willard (played brilliantly by Martin Sheen), is, "Never get out of the boat." This line was in reference to the dangers that would befall them if a member of his crew got out of the Patrol Boat River craft and entered the dense jungle surrounding Cambodia's Nung River, but it applies perfectly to numerous scenarios that befall us in the realm of self-protection. In the event of an attempted abduction, never let anyone put you in a car. Fight back as if your life depends on it, because it does! Once you become a prisoner, you no longer have control over what happens to you. Ditto for being tied up. Simply put, don't let it happen. If someone is attempting to bind you, make your stand right then and there.

SEAT BELT

Scenario

You're in the mall parking lot, just about to throw your car in gear, when your unlocked passenger door is yanked open and a carjacker gets in.

What do you do?

Tactics

The following tactics teach you how to use your seat belt both passively and aggressively to save your bacon.

Passive:

Assuming your seat belt is already locked in place, plant your foot on the accelerator and aim for a parked and unoccupied car at least 10 yards away. You want to generate sufficient force upon impact so that your unsecured and unwanted passenger will be catapulted into—and hopefully through—the windshield.

Aggressive:

1. Once the carjacker enters your car, immediately lean right, toward the intruder, cutting off the carjacker's angle of attack. Simultaneously pull the seat belt you're wearing over your head and throw it over your attacker's, then pull it down toward you. It should catch on the jacker's neck, constraining him, giving you the opportunity to grab his weapon. After looping the seat belt

around the jacker's neck stand on the gas, getting your car up to speed as quickly as possible. Aim for a large, immovable object and try to strike it head-on but more toward the passenger side. The impact will tighten the car's seat belts, whiplashing or potentially breaking your assailant's neck.

2. Instead of putting your seat belt over your foe's neck, put it over his dominant hand—usually the one holding the weapon—and use the strap's retraction to turn the tables on him.

3. With the seat belt still fastened around you, pull the cross-shoulder strap out as far as it will go—keep your car in park and your foot off the brake to allow the release—and loop it around the jacker's neck. Slam your foot on the brake and pull the belt toward you, tightening the strap down, effectively cutting off his circulation.

4. Unbuckle the seat belt and use the metal tongue as a bludgeon, targeting the jacker's hand, knee, groin, neck, or head. A direct blow to the side of the neck or temple could very well knock him unconscious.

SHOEHORN

Scenario

You're in a shoe store trying on a new pair of kicks when a robber decides he wants some new felony fliers, and he doesn't care who he has to hurt to get them.

What do you do?

Tactics

Shoehorns are almost always made out of either metal or plastic and come in two distinct sizes: the small, handheld variant or the long version, which allows you to ease your foot into the shoe without bending over. We'll cover tactics for both.

For smaller shoehorns:

1. Cup the shoehorn in your palm and use like a yawara or Kubotan (both forms of small handheld self-defense rods or sticks), or a pressure-point bludgeon. Metal variants will deliver far more telling blows, but plastic versions can still put a man down. Target the sternum, rib cage, liver, and groin.

2. Depending on the width or flare of the shoehorn, it might be a perfect fit as a wrist covering or protective gauntlet. If your assailant is armed with a knife, use the shoehorn to protect the wrist of your dominant arm against slashes as you try to take the weapon away from him.

For longer shoehorns:

1. The longer shoehorn can be used as a poke or prod stick. Depending on its composition, even a relatively blunt edge could be used as a spear point, provided it will hold up upon impact.

2. If the shoehorn is made of plastic, cut or break the edge to create a sharp or jagged point, similar to a prison shank, and stab your attacker with it.

3. If the longer shoehorn is comprised of a pliable plastic with a significant amount of bend, use it as a *sap*—a flat (or reasonably flat) lead-filled leather pouch or leather-covered metal/lead plank or stave, often 6–9 inches in length, used primarily as an impact weapon for head strikes with the goal of dazing someone or knocking him unconscious—or, if there's a small object to fling (such as a coin or rock), a microcatapult.

 GREEN BERET GUIDANCE

You've likely heard the acronym K.I.S.S., which stands for Keep It Simple, Stupid. This holds true for a variety of things, including self-defense. A simple, well-rehearsed plan has a far greater chance of succeeding than a sexy, complicated plan that you haven't walked through or practiced. And the fewer components in a plan, the smaller the chance there is of something going wrong. See, even the explanation is simple.

SHOPPING CART

Scenario

You're walking down the aisle of a grocery store when a knife-wielding psycho comes running at you, screaming about the apocalypse, which you weren't aware had begun. You hope he'll run right by you, but no, you're not that lucky. He stops directly in front of you and tells you that you're his first sacrifice to appease the blood gods.

What do you do?

Tactics

Sure, grocery shopping can be tedious, but this is one of those times when you'll be glad you have a shopping cart instead of a small carry basket.

1. Any time you're facing an armed attacker, if the opportunity presents itself to get away safely, you should take it. If your assailant is still far enough away, turn the cart around and, with one foot on the rear footrest, use it like a scooter to get away.

2. If you don't feel you can get away, charge your assailant with the shopping cart instead of racing in the opposite direction, striving for maximum speed upon impact, the intent being to hit him like an NFL linebacker and knock him flat.

3. Use the cart as a buffer, shifting directions as needed to keep the cart dead center between you and your attacker to prevent him from getting to you with the knife.

4. If your attacker is unarmed and just an angry individual seeking a confrontation, you could flip the cart over and hide beneath it. Be sure to pull your fingers inside if he attempts to strike them.

5. If you manage to get the assailant on the ground, you could flip the cart on top of him and keep him imprisoned—by either sitting or standing on the overturned cart—and wait until help arrives.

6. On some shopping carts the grab handle can be unscrewed or, if held in place by weak or thin metal, simply broken off. It can then be used as a baton or sap, either by itself or in conjunction with a ramming maneuver from the cart.

7. Flip the cart and unscrew or pull off one of the wheels. The wheel can then be used to fill out your fist for basic hand strikes (similar to a roll of quarters) or, if part of the housing rod is still attached, used like a dagger or bludgeon.

SNEAKERS/SHOES

Scenario

A casual walk takes a scary turn when you realize you're being followed. Soon, your follower closes the distance until he's directly behind you, and it's obvious an attack is imminent.

What do you do?

Tactics

Unless you live on an island or in some arctic climate where snowshoes are the norm, chances are every time you leave your home you'll be wearing shoes of some sort. Use them—along with the following tactics—to make sure you return home in one piece:

1. Before style and fashion influenced their look and composition, shoes were created and worn for one reason only—to protect your feet. That purpose carries over into the realm of self-defense. Kick with the heel or sole—wherever there is the most cushioning for your foot. A direct attack to the knee or any joint will do the job. Note:

    • If you kick with the top of the foot or instep, aim for a soft target. Striking any bone could very easily break your foot.
    • If your assailant has a knife or some other edged weapon, kicking at the offending hand can be done knowing you'll have some degree of protection.

2. If you feel more confident striking with your hands, remove your shoes and use them as protective gloves.

3. Use heavy shoes, boots, and shoes with solid heels (such as clogs) as bludgeons, aiming your kicks at sensitive or vulnerable areas (such as groin, neck, shins, and knees).

4. If your shoes have long or extended laces, remove them from all but one or two of the lace eyelets, and turn the shoe or shoes into a flail.

5. If you suffer from any sort of foot fungus, remove your shoe and press it over your assailant's mouth to cause nausea and vomiting.

6. Use the removed shoe or shoes to scoop and fling eye-irritating particles, glass shards, hot water, toxic chemicals, or acid.

SOCKS

Scenario

You're in the laundromat folding clothes when a mugger makes his move. What do you do?

Tactics

If your home doesn't have a washer and dryer in it, while it may be convenient to do your laundry late at night in a twenty-four-hour laundromat, these places are far from safe after hours, especially for women. But if you're there and in trouble, a sock should be the first object you grab, because these tactics will have you heading home in no time:

1. Stuff your keys, cellphone, loose change, or anything with some weight into the sock and knot it directly above the contents. You now have a perfectly capable flail—a handheld weapon consisting of a handle and one or more moving "heads" connected to the handle by a length of cord or chain. Be wary of objects with sharp edges. They could easily cut through the material and fall out, rendering your makeshift weapon useless.

2. If you can get a sock into your attacker's mouth, you can use it to asphyxiate your adversary—provided you get it into his mouth deep enough to fully block the airway *and* close off his nostrils.

3. Hold the sock with both hands (ends wrapped around hands or wrists) and use it to capture your enemy's arm when he strikes. A simple wrap and twist will give you control of his arm and any weapon he might be holding.

4. If you're able to get behind your adversary, use the sock like a *garrote*—a weapon used to choke or strangle (a.k.a. a handheld ligature device) using a length of wire, rope, chain, cord, or some other flexible material. Because the material will likely stretch a bit, you'll have to exert considerable force and/or hold the sock in place for at least a few minutes to render your adversary unconscious.

 EXPERT ADVICE

Because the makeshift flail is the best tactic when using a sock, you might want to consider bringing a sock with you everywhere you go. Socks take up very little room, can be kept in a pocket or purse with ease, and can be used just about anywhere with an astounding variety of contents. Equally important is the fact that there are no laws or ordinances anywhere in the world prohibiting the carry of concealed socks.

STAPLE PULLER

Scenario

You're working at your desk when an angry ex-coworker returns to the office with a gun and bad intentions.

What do you do?

Tactics

The most aggressive object on your desk is the rather diminutive staple puller, and that's what you should grab first. Use the following tactics to turn this small object into a formidable weapon of self-defense:

1. Hold the staple puller like a clamshell and use it to grab your assailant's nose, earlobe, or the webbing of his hand between his thumb and index finger. Then squeeze. Once the prongs puncture the skin, he won't be able to pull away without ripping the skin completely. Use the staple puller to control him, twisting if necessary, to make him submit.

2. Pull the staple puller open to 180 degrees, breaking the spring. Hold the center of the puller so the pronged ends protrude on either side of your clenched fist. Throw arcing punches—crosses—so the prongs strike your target instead of your fist.

3. With the staple puller opened to 180 degrees, hold one side of the pronged jaws as if you were holding a venomous snake behind its head. Strike with downward pulling motions. The idea is to hook the prongs on flesh and then rip the wound open.

4. Squeeze the staple puller closed and use it to fill out your fist like a roll of quarters. Make sure it is fully compressed upon impact, or the prongs could dig into your flesh.

5. If you've used the staple puller to remove staples from documents, gather all the staples in a pile and throw them in your assailant's face. If just one staple of the shrapnel cloud strikes his eye, the pain should be enough to distract him, giving you the upper hand.

6. Target the surface veins of your attacker's hands, feet, or arms, and try to cut them or pull them out. Obviously, the staple puller needs to be in the open position before attempting a vein grab.

T-SHIRT

Scenario

You're at a concert, and have just purchased a T-shirt commemorating the band's new album when some drunken miscreant gets in your grill.

What do you do?

Tactics

While a piece of fabric won't strike fear in anyone's eyes, when it comes to defending yourself, any object in hand is better than nothing at all. Use these tactics to make your concert T work for you:

1. Use the shirt like a hood or blindfold and throw it over your assailant's face. Then take him out with any variety of strikes, or simply use the momentary befuddlement to make your escape.

2. Wrap the shirt around your hand for protection and deck your assailant in the face.

3. Twist the shirt into a rat-tail and strike with repeated snapping motions. Wetting the tip—or coating it with Vaseline or a similar lotion—will amp up the speed, and therefore its effectiveness. A direct hit to the eye could remove the orb completely.

4. With one end of the shirt wrapped around each hand, use it like a catcher's mitt to trap your attacker's hand or foot when he strikes. Twist the fabric around your attacker's limb to exert control over the limb and ultimately control him.

5. Light the shirt on fire and throw it at your assailant.

6. Place a rock, coin, or some other small object with some heft to it amid the fabric, grab both ends, and snap it open, propelling the object at your assailant. With a little practice, you can improve your accuracy to the point that hitting a man-sized target from close range will be second nature.

 ## GREEN BERET GUIDANCE

Murphy's Law is the rule by which every member of the Special Operations community lives by. "Anything that can go wrong, will—at the worst possible opportunity." Embrace it. Accept it. And have a backup plan to counteract when ol' Mr. Murphy rears his ugly head.

TAKEOUT CONTAINER (WITH FOOD INSIDE)

Scenario

You've just picked up a takeout order from your favorite Chinese restaurant and are about to get in your car when a mugger has other ideas.

What do you do?

Tactics

Even if your assailant isn't allergic to MSG, there's still hope. Use these tactics—and your takeout—to show your assailant who's boss:

1. Open the tops of the containers and fling their contents at your attacker. Hopefully you ordered something that's piping hot. Immediately follow up by kicking, punching, or tackling the scalded mugger.

2. If the containers have those thin metal handles, tear one or two off the package and, with points facing out, strike your assailant in the neck, eyes, or ear.

3. If you have a large order, use the bag it came in like an oversized sap. A paper bag will likely break on contact so be prepared for that scenario. A plastic bag may survive beyond the first strike. If so, forget about any so-called knockout blows and aim low, below the knee, looking to sweep your attacker's feet out from under him.

4. Holding an individual container from the bottom, try to smash your takeout into your assailant's face. Open the top a bit so the contents (the hotter the better) will come out upon impact.

5. If your assailant is wearing any type of loose-fitting pants with an elastic waistband, you may be able to dump the container's contents down the front of them. If you're successful in this endeavor, ninety-nine times out of one hundred, the threat will be over.

 # THUMBTACKS

Scenario

You're at the office, tacking up a message on the communal bulletin board, when a disgruntled former coworker returns to the office with mayhem on his mind. You're the first person he encounters.

What do you do?

Tactics

Prior to any potential conflict with someone you know, you may elect to try talking that person down. Granted, this approach might just set him off further, or ruin your chance of "beating him to the punch" and taking him by surprise. Still, if there's any way to avoid a conflict and the potential violence that will ensue, take it. But assuming that's not the case, use those thumbtacks (and the following tactics) to lay down the law with your former coworker:

1. Make a fist, lick your fingers, and stick the thumbtacks to them with the points facing out! They should remain in place for at least one strike, so make it count. Any soft, exposed flesh should be the primary target, but a groin strike to a male wearing slacks, or a breast strike to a woman wearing a thin top or a single layer of outerwear, should do the job.

2. In some offices, the area around the community bulletin board will contain office supplies. Glue or tape should be among them. Use the glue or tape to secure the tacks to your hand gauntlet-style, allowing for multiple strikes without worrying about them falling off.

3. Secure the tacks to your shoes with the glue or tape, or remove your shoes and push the tack points through the fabric from the inside. Put your shoes back on and kick your attacker. The pressure of your feet against the tacks will hold them in place, and your kicks will now inflict additional pain.

4. Throw the tacks in your assailant's face, or simply throw them up in the air above your assailant's head. In most cases the aerial cloud of shrapnel will draw your attacker's attention, allowing you to mount an offensive or flee.

5. If you're being chased, throw the tacks on the ground behind you. The law of averages means some will land point up. If your attacker is barefoot or wearing thin shoes, this will stop him in his tracks. Or, if you can hide in the vicinity of where you spread the tacks, trip your assailant as he rounds a corner or races down a hall to send him flying onto the tacks, ruining his day while aiding your escape.

TOOTHBRUSH

Scenario

While on a camping trip, you're brushing your teeth in the campground's public restroom when you're confronted by a man looking to harm you. What do you do?

Tactics

Toothbrushes play a vital role in personal hygiene, but in a pinch—and with the following tactics—they can be devastating weapons:

1. Hold the toothbrush by the bristle end like a dagger and strike your opponent with the handle. It's doubtful you'll be able to punch through bone, so confine your strikes to fleshy, unprotected areas. The neck and throat are ideal, as is the femoral artery in the thigh.

2. Cut or break the toothbrush's handle to produce a point or jagged edge. This will enhance the toothbrush's ability to pierce clothing or flesh.

3. Remove the toothbrush's bristles, then palm them and throw them at your attacker to produce a distraction or blinding cloud. With your assailant distracted or temporarily blinded, run away or find and use a more potent weapon.

4. If your attacker has a firearm, you could jam the toothbrush into the gun's barrel as a last-gasp effort. Depending on the weapon's caliber and the ammo being used, this could cause the gun to explode, or at least alter the shot enough to spare your life.

5. Saturate the toothbrush's bristles with bar soap or liquid soap/hand sanitizer and introduce them into your assailant's mouth.

TOWEL

Scenario

You've just emerged from the shower at your local gym or health club when you're suddenly confronted by an angry man who wants more than your locker.

What do you do?

Tactics

Self-defense experts the world over have long been teaching average people how to defend themselves with run-of-the-mill towels. Use the tactics described here to protect yourself:

1. Tie a knot in one end of the towel and use as a *flail*—a handheld weapon consisting of a handle and one or more moving "heads" connected to the handle by a length of cord or chain. Wetting the knot will increase the weight, and therefore the swing speed.

2. Wrap the towel around your dominant hand or foot to act as a protective glove/boot for striking and kicking.

3. Wrap the towel around your weak hand and arm to use as a shield. This is the best way to take on someone armed with a knife. Even if the towel doesn't completely protect you, it will limit the depth of flesh the blade can puncture, quite possibly saving your life.

4. Use as a noose, either from the rear or by a frontal attack. Twisting the towel will tighten the fabric, allowing you to exert more pressure.

TURKEY BASTER

Scenario

You're preparing Thanksgiving dinner when a home invader breaks in, hoping to score cash and jewelry from multiple family members.

What do you do?

Tactics

This is one of those occasions when any object in hand is better than a more appropriate object that's out of reach. So grab your baster and use the following tactics to get dinner on the table on time:

1. Use the turkey baster to squirt the intruder in the face with the basting liquid. If the basting liquid is hot, it might burn your attacker's retinas, blinding him for an extended period of time (or forever), allowing you to dispatch him by any means you desire—or, if you're feeling merciful, summon the authorities. If the basting liquid is warm or cold, it could still distort his vision enough to allow you to escape or grab another more effective weapon.

2. Instead of gravy or basting liquid, fill the turkey baster with a more toxic solution. You can use soapy water, cleaning solvent, or anything that can burn or irritate the skin. You could also use gasoline, high-proof liquor, or any other flammable liquid and, after squirting your assailant, light him (or threaten to light him) on fire.

3. Ram the baster down the intruder's throat as far as possible. Although this maneuver will probably incite a gag reflex, causing his mouth to open even wider, there is the possibility he can

overcome the reflex and bite down. If that happens, squeeze the bulb forcefully, hold the baster in place, and let asphyxia do the rest.

4. Use the baster like a dagger and target soft tissue. If you bury the baster in your attacker's flesh deep enough to cause blood flow, pull the bulb off the rear of the tube and let the vacuum effect start to drain him of his vital fluids.

5. With the bulb off, use the baster like a blowgun, shooting any sharp, dart-like object small enough to fit in the tube (pin, uncurled paper clip, point of a thumbtack from a recipe corkboard, etc.). Most people have a drawer in their kitchen that contains all sorts of miscellaneous items and objects. Take a look in yours and see what you can find. Just be sure to suck in your pre-shot breath *away* from the tube's opening, otherwise you risk inhaling the dart.

GREEN BERET GUIDANCE

Have you ever noticed how cats react when they meet each other for the first time? They arch their backs, their tails stick out, and their fur puffs out. Elephants flare their ears. Gorillas puff out their chests. They make themselves look as big as possible in an attempt to let the other one know, "Hey, don't mess with me. I'm bigger than you." Animals would rather take the easy way out and avoid a fight at all costs. It's in their DNA that fights, even small ones, could result in death. There's no emergency room, trauma center, or LifeFlight airlift to patch them up, should they suffer any damage in battle. Humans are the only creatures on Earth that actually go around looking for a fight. And thanks to the miracles of science, they can keep on tempting Darwin's Law of Evolution by Natural Selection . . . until that one time they can't.

 # TV REMOTE CONTROL

Scenario

You're settled on your couch for a relaxing night of television when a home invader bursts through your front door.

What do you do?

Tactics

There's no time to hide. All you have on hand is your TV remote control. Check out these tactics to learn how to use it to save your life:

1. Use the remote control like a bludgeon. It should hold together for at least a few strikes. Aim for your attacker's joints, his temples, or the side of his neck. Rather than using a flat edge, try striking with any of the corner points. It'll make it that much easier to hit a nerve.

2. Remove the batteries and throw them at your assailant. Unless you have a world-class MLB arm, the distraction will likely be momentary, so be prepared to immediately follow up with another maneuver.

3. Remove the battery compartment door and use it to slash your attacker. Chances are it's thin and has a bit of an edge. Held between your thumb and forefinger, you should be able to generate enough force to make a slicing blow.

4. Aim the remote at your assailant and pretend it's more potent than it really is. If it's dark, you may be able to convince the invader that you're holding a gun and don't really want to shoot him, but will if he comes any closer.

TWEEZERS

Scenario

You're tweezing your eyebrows in the bathroom when you hear the breaking of glass. You exit into the hallway and find yourself staring into the eyes of a masked robber.

What do you do?

Tactics

In this instance, the tweezers in your hand—when combined with these tactics—are truly a weapon capable of maximum destruction:

1. Squeeze the tweezers closed and stab the robber directly in the eye. Even blunt tips will go through an eyeball like a hot knife through butter. And even a small pair of tweezers will probably still be long enough to reach the brain, putting an end to the robber's criminal career once and for all.

2. Reverse your grip on the tweezers so the points angle up, squeeze together and, to exert maximum force, cover all but the tips with your hand. Then use the tweezers like a shank and deliver repeated stabs to your attacker's abdomen or groin. If you can cause the robber to double over via the abdominal stabs or a kick to the groin, the side or back of his neck should be exposed and vulnerable, and is a prime target for ending this scenario.

3. Pull the tweezers apart until they are open flat, and use the extended object like a thin *shank* or *shiv*—any sharp or pointed object (usually homemade, often from an unlikely source like a

toothbrush, rolled newspaper, bar of soap, etc.) that is used to stab or slash.

4. If the robber has a gun, jam the tweezers into the firearm's barrel. The tweezers will expand a bit inside the barrel, most likely staying in place, and could cause the gun to explode upon firing.

5. This is a last-ditch tactic but, if all else fails, stick the tweezers into a socket and grab the robber with your other hand. You'll probably be electrocuted in the process, but the charge will bridge through you, shocking him as well. Hopefully you fare better than he does.

UMBRELLA

Scenario

A casual rainy-day walk down the street turns into a nightmare when a mugger tries to make you his next mark.

What do you do?

Tactics

Whether full-size or collapsible, the umbrella you're holding will make you a fan of the rain from this day forward. Use it and the following tactics to save the day:

1. Close the umbrella, reverse your grip, and use the hook on the handle to trap your assailant's arm or wrist. If your umbrella doesn't have a hook, simply strike with the handle; it will create a harder impact than striking with the canopy.

2. Open the umbrella and use as a shield. This will be effective against all hand and foot strikes, and all weapons except for firearms. If your assailant has a knife or edged weapon, allowing him to puncture the canopy may help you to trap the weapon within the metal ribs of the umbrella. As soon as the blade pierces fabric, twist or spin the umbrella to hook it.

3. Using the umbrella like a shield, strike your assailant around the opposite side of the canopy. For example, push the canopy left and come around it on the right side or vice versa. The larger the umbrella, the easier this maneuver is to accomplish.

4. Rip out the metal ribs that expand the canopy and use them as stakes or daggers. Using one rib will allow for better control, but a fistful of ribs has the potential to create more damage and, if spread apart, cover a wider area, making it harder to block all of them.

5. Jam the umbrella in your attacker's mouth and open it. This will either block his airway and asphyxiate him or cut the trachea, putting him out of commission.

6. Open the umbrella, rip off the canopy, and use the metal ribs as a grapnel or multipronged spear. You may have to bend some of the ribs outward to increase the effectiveness.

GREEN BERET GUIDANCE

Situational awareness allows you to avoid situations *before* they become situations. For example, it's late at night and you need to get home. Sure, you could walk through the park and save yourself distance and time, but don't be a fool. Spend the few dollars it'll cost to take a cab and get home safely. Also, don't be shy about asking the cabbie to keep his eye on you until you've made it to—and gone through—your door. The same mindset should apply when you're in traffic. Instead of cozying your car up to the bumper of the vehicle ahead of you, leave yourself an ample buffer. A couple of feet will do. In the event that you need to generate some speed and ram your way out of a situation, you'll have the space to do it. Live for the moment, but think a few moments ahead. *What would I do if . . . ?* The greatest chess players consider both their and their opponents' actions many moves ahead; in self-defense, even thinking just one move ahead could save your life.

WATER BOTTLE

Scenario

You're exercising in the park when a mugger tries to take more than calories away from you.

What do you do?

Tactics

Any exercise routine should always be accompanied by some means of hydration. In this case, it's a water bottle. Assuming that running away from your attacker isn't in the realm of possibility, use these tactics to put that water bottle to good use:

1. Some people prefer to freeze their water bottles prior to exercising. It prevents them from drinking the water too quickly, allowing them measured sips along the way. If that applies to you, use the frozen water bottle as a bludgeon, targeting vulnerable areas like the head and neck, or major joints like the elbows and knees.

2. Uncap the water bottle and use the spout like you would the end of a baton, jamming it into your assailant's throat, any of his pressure points, his groin, or between his ribs. The plastic will hold up under all but the most brutal impacts, and therefore should be good for any number of strikes. The size of the average water bottle's opening is perfect for rib cage strikes, and can also break the clavicle with a direct hit.

3. Pour the water over yourself, making yourself slick and hard to grab. This will make an escape easier.

4. Fill your mouth with water and spit it in your attacker's face. This is purely for distraction, and should be immediately followed up with another (more potent) tactic.

WINDSHIELD WIPER

Scenario

You return to your car parked in the lot of the local shopping mall and discover someone trying to break in. Instead of running off upon your arrival, he takes up arms against you. What do you do?

Tactics

No possession—including an automobile—is worth risking your life for. However, if you're in a situation where flight is impossible, yank the windshield wiper from its housing and use these tactics to put it to good use:

1. Swing the windshield wiper at your attacker with a wrist-flicking motion. As slashing weapons, windshield wipers can produce serious damage to soft targets. The neck and throat should be your primary targets. If you're comfortable wielding two weapons at once, you could tear off the other wiper and employ a two-handed attack.

2. Tear off the rubber cushion protecting the blade, wrap it around your fist, and use it to protect your knuckles when throwing punches. If you anticipate a lengthy fight, you could put the rubber cushion in your mouth and use as a protective mouthpiece.

3. Bend the metal wiper into a U, hold it in the center, and use it as a double-prong punch.

4. If the wiper still has the moving arm attached, swing the wiper using a basic tomahawk chopping motion. The moving arm will make it difficult for your assailant to block.

5. Bend or break the wiper into smaller lengths to be contained within your fist to improve the impact of your punches.

6. Use the end of the wiper to pry up the windshield wiper fluid hose, and fling windshield cleaner at your assailant. Get some in his eyes and you're certain to obscure his vision, if only momentarily, giving you an opportunity to mount another attack. Note: Depending on the model of car your drive, some windshield wiper fluid hoses are more readily accessible than others.

WIRE COAT HANGER

Scenario

You've just picked up your dry cleaning when a robber rushes into the store. You're in the way of his payday, and he doesn't take that lightly.

What do you do?

Tactics

In *Mommie Dearest*, Joan Crawford took issue with wire hangers. Follow her lead and use the following tactics to extricate yourself from a sticky situation:

1. Holding the hanger by the hook, swing whatever clothes it's supporting and come in behind the clothing with a kick, punch, or tackle, exactly like a matador using his cape to conceal the sword.

2. Untwist the hanger and straighten it to its full length, leaving just a small hook at the end that you can use to snag your assailant. Eyes, nose, ears, mouth—soft, vulnerable areas are the primary targets. Once your enemy is snagged, drag him down to the ground and stomp on his head or the back of his neck, or immediately employ a more effective weapon against him while he's in such a vulnerable position.

3. Wrap the hanger around your hand like a set of brass knuckles and punch your opponent. The impact will probably hurt you, but it should be even more hurtful to your foe, especially if you create points or ridges in line with your knuckles.

4. Bend and compress the metal into a pointed dagger. Even a modest point will break skin if enough force is used, or if a fleshy enough area is targeted.

5. Straighten the hanger and use as a garrote. Because the wire is far stiffer than cordage, it'll have to be pulled snug without any deviation to properly asphyxiate your attacker.

WRISTWATCH

Scenario

You're walking down the street when a mugger selects you as his personal ATM. The first thing he wants is your watch.

What do you do?

Tactics

The every-day-carry (EDC) object that gives you time of day can also be called upon to save the day, when used with the following tactics:

1. Remove your watch but, instead of handing it over, position the face over your knuckles and slug your attacker with it.

2. Smash the face of the watch with your foot or smack it against the ground. Use a piece of the broken glass or plastic as a slashing weapon: Wedge it point out between the fingers of your closed fist, or grip it between your thumb and index finger. Only a small edge is needed to get your point across (pun intended).

3. Instead of taking off the watch, grab your assailant with your watch hand and rake your hand back toward you, using the timepiece's buckle—now pressed against him—to rip his flesh.

4. If your watch is equipped with a deployant clasp—an expanding metal mechanism with two hidden clasps, usually found on expensive watches, especially top-tier diver models—use it to secure your assailant's fingers in an awkward position, and then break them.

5. Throw a punch with your watch hand, purposely aiming low. The idea is to miss the target with your fist and catch him just with the watch. Watches with larger, thicker bezels can be used to deliver the brunt of the impact.

6. Treat the watch as if it's a priceless heirloom and offer it to your assailant with care. When the criminal goes to take it, use his greed as a distraction to kick him in the groin, then immediately smash him on the base of the skull with the edge of the watch.

AFTERWORD

The purpose of this book isn't to make you paranoid. We're not trying to turn you into the kind of person who is looking over his shoulder every ten seconds, someone who must sit with his back to the wall in restaurants, or someone who continually crosses to the other side of the street whenever someone is approaching, or worse yet, refuses to leave the house. We're simply trying to remind you that we don't live in a vacuum. There are people out there who don't care about society's morals and laws. People who don't place the same value on life as you and I do. People who have no qualms hurting or killing you for financial/material gain, or to satisfy some depraved craving. Long story short, there really are monsters under the bed. But that doesn't mean you're sleeping in that bed. Hopefully, you will never have a need for the tips and lessons in this book, and the ugly stain of violence and crime will never affect you or your family.

In the meantime, make your immersion into the realm of self-protection and self-defense fun. The next time you go out with a friend or your significant other, make a game of identifying random objects—normal to obscure—and coming up with ways to defend yourself with them. See who can come up with the most ridiculous (but plausible) tactic or technique. File it away in the furthest recesses of your memory. And if that dark day comes to pass and your Jason Bourne/Jack Bauer moment arises, you'll be ready. Big time!

GLOSSARY OF TERMS

Bokken
A wooden sword used for training, usually the same size and shape as a Japanese samurai sword (a.k.a. *katana*).

Come-Along Device
Any object that can be used to grab, hook, ensnare, or lasso an enemy and force him to go where you want. If he resists, a simple twist or turn of the object will produce considerable pain, causing him to comply with your orders.

Eskrima Sticks
Also known as fighting sticks, eskrima (also spelled escrima) sticks are typically made of wood (but can be metal, fiberglass, or thermoplastic) and are wielded like batons, almost always with simultaneous or synchronized strikes.

Fist Filler
Any handheld weapon that adds more power to a barehanded punch simply by filling out your fist. A roll of quarters, small flashlight, or collapsible baton are the most common types.

Flail
A handheld weapon consisting of a handle and one or more moving "heads" that are connected to the handle by a length of cord or chain. However, any two-part or dual-section object where one section is movable can be used as a flail.

Garrote
A weapon used to choke or strangle (a.k.a. handheld ligature device). A garrote can be made of a length of wire, rope, chain, cord, or some other flexible material.

Grapnel/Grapple/Grappling Hook
A device with multiple protruding hooks, clamps, or flukes used for grasping, holding, anchoring, or dragging. Many grapnels have a rope or line attached and can be thrown, then pulled.

Hammerfist
A strike using the bottom of a tightly clenched fist, utilizing the same motion as you would swing a hammer.

Kusari-Fundo/Manriki/Manrikigusari
A Japanese handheld weapon comprised of a length of chain with a weight on each end. Some variations have spikes or blades in place of (or attached to) the weighted ends.

Neck Knife
A small knife or dagger worn around the neck, designed to be used as an emergency backup weapon.

Punji Stakes
A booby trap consisting of sharpened sticks, usually wood or bamboo, embedded in the ground pointed side up, often at the bottom of depressions or holes.

Push Dagger
A short-bladed dagger with a T-shaped handle that allows the blade to stick out past a clenched fist.

Rat-Tail
A flexible whip-like weapon comprised of a rolled towel or any reasonably soft and flexible material that is used with a backhand snapping motion: Hold one end and fling at your target, snapping it back the moment before contact to intensify the impact.

Sap
A flat (or reasonably flat) lead-filled leather pouch or leather-covered metal/lead plank or stave, often 6–9 inches in length, used primarily as an impact weapon for head strikes with the goal of dazing someone or knocking him unconscious.

Shank/Shiv
Any sharp or pointed object—usually homemade, often from an unlikely source (toothbrush, rolled newspaper, bar of soap)—used to stab or slash.

Truncheon
A baton, bludgeon, or billy club, often carried by a police officer or prison guard.

INDEX

Action, committing to, 96

Aerosol can, as weapon, 13

Alertness, 31

Antenna, as weapon, 42–43

The Art of War (Sun Tzu), 68

Ashtray, as weapon, 15–16

Avoiding violence, 68, 189, 194

Bad guys, thinking like, 79

Bag, plastic/garbage, as weapon, 137–38

Bag of dog poop, as weapon, 17–18

Balls as weapons

    billiard ball, 25–26

    bowling ball, 34–35

Barrette/bobby pin, as weapon, 19–20

Baseball cap, as weapon, 21–22

Baster, as weapon, 188–89

Billfold, as weapon, 23–24

Billiard ball, as weapon, 25–26. *See also*
  Cue stick

Blanket, as weapon, 27–28

Board, as weapon, 11–12

Book of matches, as weapon, 29

Book overview, 8, 202

Bottles as weapons

    hot sauce bottle, 30–31

    water bottle, 195

Bouquet of flowers, as weapon, 32–33

Bowling ball, as weapon, 34–35

Broom, as weapon, 36–37

Brushes as weapons

    hairbrush, 99–100

    toothbrush, 186

Candle, as weapon, 38–39

Candy bar, as weapon, 40–41

Cans as weapons

    aerosol can, 13

    garbage can, 92–93

    oil can, 149–50

Cap, as weapon, 21–22

Car, never getting put in, 168

Car antenna, as weapon, 42–43

Car keys, as weapon, 44–45

Cart, shopping, as weapon, 173–74

Casino chips, as weapon, 143–44

Cellphone, as weapon, 46–47

Ceramic plate, as weapon, 48–49

Chain, as weapon, 50–51

Chips (poker/casino), as weapon, 143–44

Chopsticks, as weapon, 52–53

Clipboard, as weapon, 54–55

Close Quarters Battle (CQB) principles,
  122

Coat hanger, as weapon, 198–99

Coffee mug, as weapon, 56–57

Coffeepot, as weapon, 58–59

Coins, as weapon, 103–4, 159–60

Collar, dog leash and, 72–73

Comb, as weapon, 60

Committing to action, 71, 96

Compact, as weapon, 145–46

Computer, as weapon, 111–12

Confrontations. *See* Self-defense

Cord, as weapon, 78–79

Corkscrew, as weapon, 61–62

Crazy, going, 112

Crutches, as weapon, 63–64

Cue stick, as weapon, 65–66. *See also*
  Billiard ball

Decisiveness, 39, 96
Defendu fighting system, 154
Diaper, as weapon, 67–68
Dish soap, as weapon, 69
Disposable razor, as weapon, 70–71
Dog leash, as weapon, 72–73
Dog poop, as weapon, 17–18
Drinking straw, as weapon, 74–75
Duct tape, as weapon, 76–77

Electrical cord, as weapon, 78–79. *See also* Jumper cables
Electrical tape, as weapon, 76–77
Emery board, as weapon, 121–22
Environment, knowing, 12
Extension cord, as weapon, 78–79
Eyeglasses, as weapon, 80

Fight, avoiding, 68, 189, 194
Fighting, reason/inspiration for, 136
Fighting hard, 39, 104, 112, 122
File, nail, as weapon, 121–22
Fire extinguisher, as weapon, 82–83
Flashlight, as weapon, 84–85
Flowers, as weapon, 32–33
Focusing, 150
Food containers, as weapon, 135–36, 183
Fork, as weapon, 86–87
Frisbee, as weapon, 88–89
Frying pan, as weapon, 90–91

Garbage bag, as weapon, 137–38
Garbage can, as weapons, 92–93
Glasses (eye/sun), as weapon, 80
Glossary of terms, 203
Golf
    bags as weapons, 94–95
    balls as weapons, 95–96
    clubs as weapons, 95
    shoes as weapons, 96

tees as weapons, 95–96
Green Beret guidance
    avoiding violence, 68, 189, 194
    being alert, 31
    being prepared, 87
    committing to action, 71, 96
    CQB principles, 122
    Defendu fighting system, 154
    embracing Murphy's Law, 182
    fighting hard, 39, 104, 112, 122
    focusing, 150
    going crazy, 112
    keeping it simple, 172
    knowing environment, 12
    knowing risks, 79
    making a stand, 71
    motor skills and fighting, 144
    never get put in car, 168
    Observe, Orient, Decide, Act, 39
    reason to fight, 136
    Reptile Brain awareness, 18
    robbery foiled example, 55
    screaming, 112, 116
    situational awareness, 194
    staring them down, 156
    street fight mentality, 47
    Surprise, Speed, Violence of Action, 122
    thinking like bad guys, 79
Green Beret way, 9–10
Guitar, as weapon, 97–98

Hairbrush, as weapon, 99–100
Hammer, as weapon, 101–2
Handful of coins, as weapon, 103–4
Hanger, as weapon, 198–99
High heels, as weapon, 105–6
Hot sauce bottle, as weapon, 30–31

Ice scraper, as weapon, 107–8
Indecisiveness, 96
Intuition, warning you, 18

Jumper cables, as weapon, 109–10

Keys, as weapon, 44–45

Laptop computer, as weapon, 111–12
Leash, as weapon, 72–73
Leopard, woman defeating, 104
Light bulb, as weapon, 113–14
Lighter, as weapon, 115–16
Lipstick/lip balm, as weapon, 117–18
Loved ones, fighting for, 136
Lumber, as weapon, 11–12

Matches, as weapon, 29
Mirrors as weapons
    compact/powder puff, 145–46
    handheld mirror, 119–20
    rearview mirror, 151–52
Mitt, oven, as weapon, 125–26
Mop, as weapon, 36–37
Motor skills and fighting, 144
Mug, as weapon, 56–57
Murphy's Law, embracing, 182

Nail file, as weapon, 121–22
Necktie, as weapon, 166
Newspaper, as weapon, 123–24

Observe, Orient, Decide, Act, 39
Oil can, as weapon, 149–50
Oven mitt, as weapon, 125–26

Paddle, Ping-Pong, as weapon, 133–34
Pan, as weapon, 90–91
Paper, as weapon
    newspaper, 123–24
    toilet paper roll, 153–54
Paper clip, as weapon, 127–28
Pen/pencil, as weapon, 129–30
Pillow/pillowcase, as weapon, 131–32
Pin, safety, as weapon, 161–62

Ping-Pong paddle, as weapon, 133–34
Pipe, PVC, as weapon, 147–48
Pizza box (with pizza), as weapon,
    135–36
Plastic bag, as weapon, 137–38
Plate, as weapon, 48–49
Plunger, as weapon, 139–40
Pocketbook, as weapon, 141–42
Poker chips, as weapon, 143–44
Poop, as weapon, 17–18, 67–68
Powder puff, as weapon, 145–46
Preparedness, 87
Purse (pocketbook), as weapon, 141–42
PVC pipe, as weapon, 147–48

Quart of oil, as weapon, 149–50

Razor, as weapon, 70–71
Rearview mirror, as weapon, 151–52
Remote control, as weapon, 190
Reptile Brain, 18
Risks, knowing, 79
Robbery foiled example, 55
Rolling pin, as weapon, 155–56
Roll of toilet paper, as weapon, 153–54
Rope, as weapon, 157–58
Rubber band, as weapon, 159–60
Rules, fighting without, 47

Safety pin, as weapon, 161–62
Salad tongs, as weapon, 163–64
Salt, as weapon, 165
Scarf, as weapon, 166
Scraper, ice, as weapon, 107–8
Screaming, 112, 116
Scuba tank, as weapon, 167–68
Seat belt, as weapon, 169–70
Self-defense. *See also* Green Beret
    guidance; *specific weapons*
    arming yourself, 7–8
    Green Beret way, 9–10

striking first, 35
this book and, 8, 203
violent crime and, 7
Shirt, as weapon, 181–82
Shoehorn, as weapon, 171–72
Shoes as weapons
high heels, 105–6
sneakers/other, 175–76
Shopping cart, as weapon, 173–74
Simplicity, importance of, 172
Situational awareness, 194
Sneakers, as weapon, 175–76
Soap, as weapon, 69
Socks, as weapon, 177–78
Standing up to violence, 71
Staple puller, as weapon, 179–80
Staring them down, 156
Straw, as weapon, 74–75
Street fight mentality, 47
Stress, reacting under, 112, 144
Striking first, 35
Sunglasses, as weapon, 80
Surprise, Speed, Violence of Action, 122

Tacks, as weapon, 184–85
Takeout containers (with food), as
weapons, 135–36, 183

Tape, as weapon, 76–77
Thinking like bad guys, 79
Thumbtacks, as weapons, 184–85
Tie (necktie), as weapon, 166
Toilet paper roll, as weapon, 153–54
Tongs, salad, as weapon, 163–64
Toothbrush, as weapon, 186
Towel, as weapon, 187
T-shirt, as weapon, 181–82
Turkey baster, as weapon, 188–89
TV remote control, as weapon, 190
Tweezers, as weapon, 191–92
2 x 4, as weapon, 11–12

Umbrella, as weapon, 193–94

Van, never getting put in, 168
Voice, as weapon, 116

Wallet, as weapon, 23–24
Warning, inner, 18
Watch, as weapon, 200–201
Water bottle, as weapon, 195
Windshield wiper, as weapon, 196–97
Wire coat hanger, as weapon, 198–99
Wristwatch, as weapon, 200–201

ABOUT THE AUTHORS

Master Sergeant Terry Schappert is a twenty-two-year veteran of the United States Army, most of it in Special Forces. He left the military in 1997 and came back after 9/11, and he's still in—still fighting the fight. His early career saw him as a Ranger-qualified 82nd Airborne Division paratrooper in the Gulf War, and the rest of his time has been as a Green Beret medic and team sergeant. He's been deployed on combat and training missions around the world, and has no idea what he's going to do when he finally puts down his rucksack and rifle. Terry has also been lucky enough to do several TV shows: *Warriors* on the History Channel, *Shark Attack Survival Guide* for the Discovery Channel's Shark Week, *CQB* in the Czech Republic, and two seasons of *Dude, You're Screwed* on the Discovery Channel. Some might call it an interesting life; Terry just says he's lazy and would never be able to have a real job.

Adam Slutsky has *none* of Terry Schappert's qualifications. But what Adam lacks in skill, he makes up for in experience—although it's usually on the *wrong* end of the experience. As a former participatory journalist for some of the planet's hippest men's lifestyle publications, Adam has taken part in a multitude of high-octane activities to provide his readers with the truest sense of the action. He's been shot, stabbed, tased, stun-gunned, sapped, brass-knuckled, choked out, knocked out, body-slammed, roundhouse-kicked, and beaten up in virtually every fighting style known to man, by amateur and expert pugilists of every possible age and description. For this book, he served as Terry's flesh-and-bone test dummy. The scars he's acquired—both mental and physical—are for you.